SHERMAN F. MORGAN's

CLASSIC AVIATION HUMOR

BOOK II

Pendragon Publishing Co.
1484 Old Tara Lane
Ft. Mill, S.C. 29715

First Edition, September 1989

Printed and bound in the United States of America.

Library of Congress Catalog Card Number:
89-92018

International Standard Book Number:
0-944792-01-4

Also By Sherman F. Morgan

The Aviation Humor of 1987
The Little Apple Orchard
Good Sticks

Acknowledgements

So many people took advantage of my invitation in *The Aviation Humor of 1987* to send stories from all over the world, that it would be impossible to name all of them here. Wherever possible, I tried to include their names directly in the story, whenever I used a piece of the material that they sent to me. Thanks so much to all of you, this book would not have been written without your generous contributions.

The book also would never have been completed without the on-going help of Bob Reimard of the Alamo Aviation Art Gallery, and Ed Dingivan. Both proved to be invaluable proof readers.

The very talented Tina Brown Farney of Charlotte, N.C. created the cover of the book, as well as an illustration for nearly every story. Captain Eddie Hoffman and Greg Thompson of US Air also made invaluable contributions with their art work. Mike Henderson of Homer City, Pennsylvania also created an excellent illustration for the story, "Men With the Bark On".

The most fun I had while writing this book was collecting the stories. You have no idea how good it made me feel to open my mail and find a new story there—or get a phone call or a face-to-face narration of a good yarn.

The only thing that felt as good as receiving the new stories, was reading the letters of appreciation for the first humor book. Thanks so much to everyone who took the time to send those—they provided a great deal of encouragement for writing this book.

Dedication

These laughs are dedicated to the guy who made me laugh more than anyone else ever has — my brother, Michael Leland Morgan.

Mike was eleven months and three days younger than me. No matter how bad things sometimes seemed to our adolescent minds while we were growing up, Mike could always make me laugh. My childhood would have been a lonely bore without him.

We slept together from the time Mike left his cradle until I left home, immediately after High School.

Mike was killed in Jakarta, Indonesia on the 13th of July, 1989. He was 33.

My thoughts of Mike now, always end with a smile.

Foreword

Well, here we are, in a brand new decade. This foreword is being written in the first hour of the year of our Lord, 1990. What a decade the '80s were—what a decade we expect the '90s to be!

This book, is of course, a sequel to *The Aviation Humor of 1987*. When I finished that book, I appealed to its readers to send me their best stories, with the intention of writing an annual sequel to the first book. Well, with the admission that this foreword is being written in the first minutes of 1990—it's obvious that *The Aviation Humor of 1988* never made it to the market. But that's all right. There were plenty of good reasons for the delay.

One reason was, that a couple of more urgent books required my attention. My novel, *Good Sticks,* ate up a good portion of the time that could have been devoted to *The Aviation Humor of 1988*. But, I needed to get *Good Sticks* down on disk while its concept was still fresh in my mind.

Likewise, a children's book which we brought to market in October of 1989 titled, *The Little Apple Orchard* seemed to assume a more urgent priority than this humor sequel. The future will tell whether its introduction had the positive influence on commercial aviation that we hoped for.

A few, more personal reasons, also interposed, such as the decision to transfer my airline flying from US Air's Pittsburgh domicile, to the Charlotte hub. That, in turn, drove the decision to leave my C-5 Air Force Reserve squadron in San Antonio. We have moved to the Carolinas, where I am now a C-130 pilot in the Air National Guard unit located in Charlotte, North Carolina. (Every story in this book except one was written prior to my departure from San Antonio).

The bottom line (or paragraph) of this foreword, should emphasize the fact, that we intend to continue this sequel of Aviation Humor books—and we thus continue to solicit your contributions. More urgent projects may delay its immediate publication, but you can rest assured that Classic Aviation Humor—Book III is *already* an ongoing project. W*e need your contributions.*

Thank you for your patronage—especially those of you who sent checks for this book immediately after reading The Aviation Humor of 1987 (and before this book was even written!).

I hope that this title provides the laughs you desire—and I pray that the '90s provide the adventure, challenge, and fulfillment that all of us deserve.

Men With The Bark On

My favorite piece of art work was painted by the great American western painter, Frederic Remington. He finished it in circa (1889), and called it, *My Bunky*.

Remington had an eye for men of action, direct men — the straight-forward breed that he referred to as, "Men with the bark on." I also enjoy the company of these men, although they can at times, provide experiences which are as harrowing as they are entertaining. A friend of mine recently told me of an experience he had, which emphasizes this point nicely.

My friend's name is Tom (he asked me not to print his last name) and his story involves an incident which occurred 8 years ago while he was flying as first officer for a captain, whom we shall call, "Bill."

Tom approached me one day in the crew room at Pittsburgh, and said, "Listen, I have this great story that I've been wanting to tell you ever since I read your first book, but I had to wait until Bill retired. He has a terrible temper. But, he is retired and lives in Hawaii now, so I don't think I have anything to worry about."

Tom said that Bill was a fat, bald, mean old guy, who marched around airports wearing a captain's uniform and making life miserable for the people who had to be around him. Bill had an exceptionally short fuse, and a mean temper to boot. If it's true that the only thing meaner than a pit bull with AIDS, is the guy who gave it to him, then Bill would have to be that guy.

For three days, Tom and the flight engineer on their 727 had watched Bill chew out every ticket agent, flight attendant, cleaner, and ground handler who had been unfortunate enough to cross paths with Bill. Tom and the engineer were getting pretty tired of not having any company in the cockpit, but they couldn't blame the flight attendants for staying away.

"Oh well," they thought, *"today is the last day of the trip. If we can just put up with him for two more legs, we'll be home free."*

Unfortunately they were not to be so lucky — when they landed in Boston on the next to the last leg of the trip, they discovered that the ground handlers were conducting a work slow down. It seemed to take forever before a marshaller showed up to park them at their gate, which of course gave Bill all the reason he needed to fly into a tantrum.

Bill ranted and raved in the cockpit while the Boston passengers disembarked, and the new passengers boarded for Pittsburgh. Tom

7

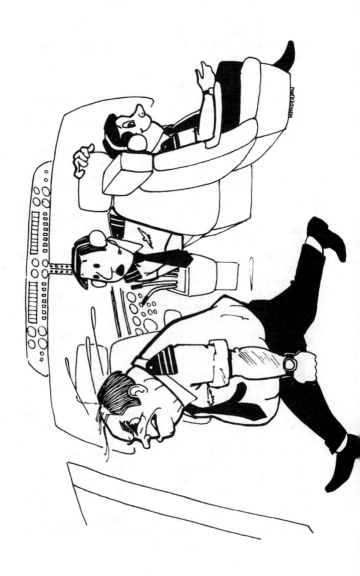

and the engineer got their clearance to PIT (Pittsburgh) and prepared the airplane for the flight, all the while secretly wondering if Bill would work himself up enough to have a heart attack before they left.

Finally, all the passengers were boarded, they had all the necessary paperwork, all of the doors were closed, and the jet way had been pulled away from the airplane — but there was no push crew in sight to push them back away from the gate.

Tom could see what was coming, so he thought, *"maybe the ground handlers are plugged in downstairs, and they're just waiting for us to call them before they step out from the shade of the fuselage."*

So, Tom pressed down the intercom button on the radio control box mounted on his side console, and quickly keyed his microphone twice to get the attention of anyone listening to the intercom outside.

Unfortunately, the entire push crew was still inside their break room drinking coffee, so no one was plugged into the external intercom jack to hear Tom's double clicks.

Bill had been indulging himself with a dissertation on the incompetence of the ground handling personnel, when *he* heard Tom's double clicks on the intercom channel.

Bill naturally assumed that the clicks had come from a ground handler outside the airplane, so he snatched his microphone off it's hook and barked, "The damned brakes are off and *we're* ready to push."

After a few seconds went by with no reply, Tom realized what had happened. It was too good an opportunity to pass up, so Tom sneaked the mike back up beside the right side of his face so Bill wouldn't notice him, and said, "Look you fat old bastard, we'll push you when we're good and ready."

Bill jumped so high in his seat that the seat belt nearly snapped. Bill immediately turned to Tom and said, "Did you hear that?"

Tom had lowered his mike by then, so he turned innocently to Bill and said, "Did I hear what?"

Bill said, "Did you hear what that ground handler said to me?"

Tom said, "I didn't hear anything Bill — I have my intercom box set up for talking to ground control — I'm not listening to the intercom channel at all."

Bill grabbed his mike again and shouted into it, "What the hell did you say to me?"

By this time Tom was acting like he was trying to look over the nose of the airplane to see if he could spot the culprit cowering outside, but of course in reality he was simply using the ruse to turn his head away and shield the mike so he could reply, "I said you fat bald old jerk — if you come down here, I'm going to kick your butt!"

Well, that was too much for Bill to take. He jerked off his seat belt and slammed his seat against the back stops, then stormed out of the cockpit so he could lower the air stairs and confront his tormentor.

It was all the engineer could do to keep a straight face until Bill was out of the cockpit — he had seen and heard everything that Tom had done. As soon as the cockpit door slammed shut, Tom turned around to exchange looks with the engineer. What a fitting pay-back for the crap they had put up with for the past 3 days!

They were still grinning and slapping their knees, waiting for Bill to march back through the door wearing an, "I've been had," expression on his face, when the senior flight attendant waved her arm inside the door to warn them that he was returning. As soon as Bill stepped into the cockpit, Tom's smile disappeared.

Bill's tie was pulled open and wrenched over to the side of his neck, and a tiny trickle of blood was streaming down from the corner of his mouth. He slumped into his seat and started fumbling for the ends of his seat belt, and Tom could see that both of his eyes were puffy and starting to turn black.

The engineer finally asked in his most sincere voice, "What happened out there Bill?"

Bill mumbled, "Just what I expected — the big jerk *acted* like he didn't even know why I was hitting him at first."

Well, the ground handler was apparently just as frightened by the incident as Bill was. For months Bill waited for a call from the chief pilot's office to explain why he had assaulted a member of the push crew at Boston, but the ground handler never reported it.

The slow down at Boston ended that very day (a fact which Bill always took credit for in private quarters) and Tom secretly savored the sweet revenge he had extracted. And the flight engineer? Well, if Tom was in the room, that engineer never had to pay for another cup of coffee until the day Bill retired and moved out of town.

Mixed Company

How many times have you been caught right in the middle of a good story in the hotel van, when a couple of nonairline- employee passengers hop onboard? My old DC-9 classmate, Scott Theuer, has come up with the perfect joke to tell during these "mixed company" sessions.

Whenever Scott finds himself in this predicament, he just smiles at the "A" flight attendant and says, "Have you ever flown with Jim Gorman? He's a captain on the 737-300."

Regardless of whether she says that she knows Jim or not, Scott says, "Did you hear that story about Jim talking to the kid on the moped while he was driving his brand new Porsche home?"

If she smiles obligingly, Scott tells her the story about the day that Jim pulled up to a stoplight in his brand new Porsche and looked over at a youngster sitting on a moped in the lane next to him. The moped was a top-of-the-line custom model, with turn signals, chrome fenders and a dual-beam headlight.

Jim said, "Nice moped you have there buddy."

The bow-tie bedecked youngster glanced over at the hot-off-the-showroom-floor Porsche and said, "Thanks mister — that's a beautiful car you're driving."

Jim said, "Thanks, I just picked it up from the dealer, I'm driving it home for the first time right now."

The kid said, "Wow, that's neat. Look at that slick metal-flake paint job and those sexy mag wheels — man that's a great looking car."

Jim smiled and said, "Thanks," and then to his surprise, the kid leaned his moped over and stuck his head inside the driver's window of the Porsche.

The kid said, "Wow, look at that interior. Plush, deep-pile carpeting and leather seats — and dig that graphic equalizer on the stereo CD player. Man, this is a great car!"

Jim was relieved when the kid finally extracted his head and leaned his moped upright again — away from his car. When he glanced up at the traffic light, Jim saw that the red light had turned to green.

"Time *to show this lad what a Porsche will do,*" he thought, so Jim winked toward the kid and said, "Hang in there kid — someday you'll have one of these too."

With that, Jim mashed the accelerator pedal to the floorboard and left it there until the Porsche was in 4th gear and accelerating through 100 mph. He wanted to see the expression on the kid's face (a scant 1/4 mile behind him) so he glanced in his rear-view mirror. To his amazement, he saw the headlight of the moped accelerating toward him!

Before Jim could react, the moped rocketed past him! He immediately shifted into 5th gear and set out after the moped's retreating taillight.

Jim kept the gas pedal nailed to the floor — he was determined to catch up to the moped, which was now so far ahead of him that its taillight had disappeared. He strained to catch a glimpse of the dim taillight, but to his astonishment — he saw the moped's headlight racing back toward him!

The moped rocketed past Jim's Porsche in the opposite direction — the kid was moving so fast when he went by that all Jim could see was a blur of color. Jim glanced down at his speedometer — he was doing 190 mph!

He was just about to turn around and take off after the moped in the opposite direction, when Jim noticed a headlight in his rear-view mirror. *It was the moped again!* But this time, instead of approaching from the passing lane, the headlight seemed to be racing up directly behind the Porsche.

The headlight grew larger and larger until... **WHAM!** *The light slammed into the back of the Porsche!*

Jim immediately started downshifting and braking, but it took almost 5 miles to bring the Porsche to a complete stop. When he finally had the car pulled over to the side of the road, he jumped out and ran back to see if he could help the kid.

He found the kid sprawled on top of the mangled moped — his clothes were torn to shreds and and his body was covered with scrapes and bruises.

Jim said, "Oh my gosh — is there anything I can do for you kid?"

The kid opened one of his blackened eyes and said, "Well... you could start by unhooking my suspenders from your mirror."

That story always reminds me of the tale about the ex-fighter pilot flying a DC-9 between Allentown and Wilkes-Barre, Pennsylvania.

This story was mailed to me by an airline captain who wished to remain anonymous, so we'll just identify him as Bill. Bill is domiciled in Minneapolis, and he sent this story to me after reading my first aviation humor book.

Bill said that about ten years ago, he was flying a DC-9 trip with a brand new first officer named Jeff. Jeff had flown F-16s in the Air Force before going to work for Bill's airline, and he still had a little bit of that aggressive, fighter pilot mentality.

The trip went from Minneapolis to Allentown, then hopped up to Wilkes-Barre. After Wilkes-Barre they flew right back down to Allentown and then back to Minneapolis. Wilkes-Barre is only 80 miles northwest of Allentown, so the leg was only scheduled for 16 minutes block-to-block.

The captain customarily flies the first leg of each trip, so Bill flew to Allentown where their first load of passengers disembarked. As soon as the Allentown passengers were off the airplane, the ticket agent strolled into the cockpit with the weight and balance sheet for the leg to Wilkes-Barre.

The agent said, "I'm not putting anyone on for Wilkes-Barre, so you guys can takeoff whenever you want. I'll see you in a half hour on your way back to Minne."

Well, what the agent was saying of course was that he wasn't putting any *new* passengers on the airplane for the leg to Wilkes-Barre. Unfortunately, what Jeff thought the agent was saying, was that all the passengers had gotten off in Allentown, and no new ones were getting on for the flight to Wilkes-Barre.

Working under this false impression (that the only people in the cabin for the next leg would be the 3 flight attendants) Jeff thought, *"All right, here's my chance to really impress the girls!"*

The wind was blowing out of the south, so Bill taxied the DC-9 to runway 24. The tower cleared them to hold in position on the runway, so Bill lined up the airplane on the runway and set the parking brake, then said, "Your airplane."

Jeff smiled mischievously and said, "My airplane."

The tower cleared them to take off, and Jeff advanced the throttles. Airline pilots normally release the brakes before they advance the power, but Jeff left the parking brake set while he spooled both engines up. Bill was just about to tell him to release the parking brake, when Jeff tapped the rudder pedals and the brakes released.

The airplane immediately started racing down the 7,600 foot runway and Bill thought, *"I have to remember to say something to him about that later."*

As soon as the wheels lifted off the runway Jeff said, "Gear up," and immediately raised the gear handle.

Bill thought, *"After I tell him not to make standing takeoffs, I*

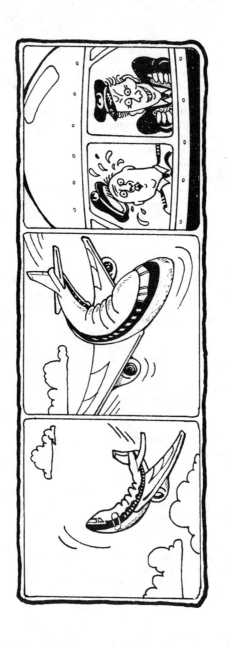

need to tell him to let the airplane climb a little higher before raising the gear."

Since Wilkes-Barre lies northwest of Allentown, their climb out instructions called for a right turn to 300 degrees. Bill expected Jeff to climb to at least 400 feet above the airport, and then begin a gentle climbing right turn. Instead, as soon as the gear started coming up, Jeff racked the airplane over into a 60 degree bank and pulled back hard on the yoke!

Bill was still making a mental note to tell Jeff to wait until 400 feet to begin his climb out turns, when he saw the attitude indicator passing through the 30 degree bank index. When the angle of bank kept going past 45 degrees and then approached 60, Bill decided to take control of the airplane.

Unfortunately, before Bill could get his hands on the yoke, Jeff pulled it back hard into his lap and loaded the airplane up with 4 Gs!

Bill's chin fell down to his chest, and his nice, wide field of vision started choking down until all he could see was a narrow little tunnel with dark edges that led straight down to the attitude indicator.

In the back, all 23 elderly lady members of the Wilkes-Barre historical quilting society, had been rubbing the back of their necks after Jeff's sling-shot standing take off. With 4 Gs pressing them down into their seats, the ladies decided that it was a good time to take a little nap.

When the heading indicator approached 300 degrees, Jeff rolled the DC-9 out of its steep bank, then lowered the nose to allow the airplane to level off at 6,000 feet. The throttles were still set at take off power however, so the airplane quickly accelerated toward 350 knots.

Bill's vision started returning to him as soon as the airplane returned to 1 G flight. As soon as he felt he had recovered enough to fly, Bill grabbed the controls and barked, **"MY AIRPLANE!"**

Jeff laughed and said, "Yea, you fly a minute, will you? I want to give the girls a good PA."

Bill was astonished to see Jeff wink at him, and then reach for the PA (Public Address) microphone. Bill started to stop him, but then he realized that their airspeed was 100 knots too fast for their altitude! So, instead of saying something to Jeff, he pulled both throttles to idle and extended the speed brake. While Bill was busy flying, Jeff snatched the microphone off the back of the radio console and brought it up to his mouth.

Their little old hearts had just managed to pump enough blood back up to their brains to revive them, when the ladies in the back heard Jeff's voice over the PA system... *"Hey — one of you lazy whores bring me a damn cup of coffee!"*

Needless to say, young Jeff learned his lesson about language in mixed company the hard way. I hope he is doing well in his new line of employment.

Of course, as Jeff found out, profanity is a thing to be avoided regardless of who is around, but an employee in uniform has to be doubly careful about such things. I received a letter the other day from the chief pilot of a commuter airline on the west coast, which amply reinforces this principle. (The chief pilot wished to remain anonymous.)

It seems that the chief pilot received an irate letter from a lady passenger, who wrote that she had been offended by a torrential string of obscenities emanating from the cockpit of one of the company's airplanes while the passengers were boarding. The letter specified the date, time, and flight number of the incident, so it was a simple matter for the chief pilot to research the maintenance log and find out which mechanics were on duty that day.

The chief pilot made a copy of the lady's letter and forwarded it to the most senior mechanic involved, along with a note asking for a reply to the lady's letter. A couple of days later, he received a response from the mechanic, which read:

Me and Bill was on the job on the day in question. We was working on a busted electrical wire in the cockpit. Bill was holding the wire while I soldered on it, and I accidentally let some of the molten lead fall. It went down Bill's sock.

Bill turned to me and said, "You really must be more careful Harry," and I said, "Indeed, I must Bill. I will see that it don't happen again."

Indeed — it's important to behave oneself in mixed company.

Mothers, Roosters, and the Red Sox

Mike Sibbald was the commander of the 326th MAS (Military Airlift Squadron) the first time I met him. The 326th is one of the two C-5 reserve squadrons at Dover AFB, Delaware, but that isn't really very important for the purposes of this story — but Mike Sibbald certainly is.

Mike was originally born in Scotland, and he certainly didn't have any difficulty putting on his Scottish brogue when it suited his purposes. As a matter of fact, Mike had no trouble affecting practically any dialect he wished — since the everyday English he spoke around us was a "learned tongue."

I got a kick out of a story that one of our other Dover pilots, Larry Mercker, told us about a flight he took to Europe and back with Mike. The story goes, that on their way home from Germany, Mike was operating the radios while Larry concentrated on setting up the triple inertial navigation systems for their "coast out fix" off the west coast of England.

They were under the air traffic control of Macrihanish center at the time, and... like any good American boy raised in the deep South or Boston who suddenly finds himself talking to an old neighbor... Mike was rapidly slipping back into his native tongue.

Larry said that he looked over at the right seat a couple of times after Mike said something to the Macrihanish controller — half expecting to see "Scotty" of the Star Ship Enterprise sitting there.

Finally the Macrihanish controller couldn't take the suspense any longer, so he said, "Hey MAC 123, ye sound like ye might 'ave spent some time in my neighborhood."

Mike answered, "Aye Macrihanish, I 'ave — I was born just down the road a little ways from where ye're sittin."

The Macrihanish controller said, "Is that so now — do ye 'ave any family left there?"

Mike said, "Aye, I 'ave — me dear old mother still lives in the 'ouse I was born in."

The Macrihanish controller said, "Is that a fact — do you know if she as a telly?"

Mike said, "Aye, she does indeed."

The Macrihanish controller said, "Might she be interested in a short phone patch conversation with ye tonight?"

Mike said, "Well, she just might be at that now."

The Macrihanish controller said, "Fine, if ye'll give me her

number, I'll ring her up and see what we can arrange."

Mike said, "That's very kind of ye mate," and gave the controller his mother's phone number.

Of course by now Larry and the rest of the crew were mesmerized by Mike's antics — thoughts of coast-out-fixes and position reports were long forgotten.

As a matter of fact, the other aircraft in the sector weren't missing the ramifications of what was happening either. The normally-congested frequency stayed completely silent for nearly several minutes—everyone postponed their requests and reports so they wouldn't interfere with the phone patch.

Finally, the silence was broken by the center controller's call, "MAC 123, this is Macrihanish — are ye still there?"

Mike answered, "Aye Macrihanish, we're standing by."

The Macrihanish controller answered, "Well MAC, I rang up your mother, and when she answered the telly I told 'er that it was Macrihanish air traffic control center callin, and that I 'appened to know that her finest son was flyin over 'ead at 35,000 feet — and I just wondered if there was something that she might be wanting to say to you..."

After several seconds of silence on the radio, Mike pressed his transmit button and said, "What 'appened then Macrihanish?"

The controller finally said, "She just said, 'Aye — tell him to keep down the damn noise,' and then she hung up on me!"

Listening to Mike tell stories, was even better than listening to other people tell stories about Mike. Mike had dozens of great tales, but I'm sure the one he got the most simultaneous guffaws with in mixed company... was the Benbow rooster story. The first time I heard him tell it was the night Mike was invited to speak at Benbow's change-of-command ceremony at the Dover AFB Officer's Club.

The outgoing commander, Colonel Benbow, was a popular C-5 squadron commander who originally hailed from northern Maine. The story centers around a trip Benbow took to see his parents in his old home town.

Benbow decided to drive to Maine from Delaware, which of course meant that he had to traverse New Hampshire. Normally the thought of driving through New Hampshire would have worried Benbow, since New Hampshirites had an uncanny knack for detecting anyone from Maine in their midst, and quickly making life miserable for them.

But, Benbow decided that his years in the Air Force would

camouflage his speech and mannerisms sufficiently to prevent any harassment, so he elected to not only drive through the state — he even decided to risk eating there!

When breakfast time came, Benbow selected a quaint little diner just outside one of the small New Hampshire towns along the road, and he pulled in for a quick bite.

The people inside the diner acted wary of Benbow, but they were too unsure of his true origin to give him any trouble — too unsure that is, until he ordered 3 scrambled eggs with plenty of hot sauce on them.

You see, in New Hampshire, customers pay for their breakfasts by the egg, so any true New Hampshirite will always order his eggs fried or boiled, so he can count them and make certain he is getting his money's worth.

As soon as the waitress reported the order, the diner's owner realized that Benbow was a wayward "Maineiac," so he told his cook, "Feed him rotten eggs."

The waitress whispered the plan to the other customers while she moved among them to refill their coffee cups, so everyone was looking forward to the expression on Benbow's face when he bit into those eggs.

Benbow took his time about buttering his toast when the waitress delivered his breakfast — he knew that all the other customers were watching him, but he couldn't imagine why. The hot sauce effectively masked the eggs' odor, until he slipped the first forkfull onto his tongue.

Instantly, Benbow realized the reason for all the wide-eyed expectant grins around him — they were waiting for him to blanch and spit the putrid eggs from his mouth.

Instead, Benbow straightened his back, chewed twice, and forced down the mouthful — quickly but deliberately chasing it with a long drink from his coffee mug.

With the taste of the eggs washed away and his dignity still intact, Benbow was ready to turn his attention to the obvious perpetrator of the incident.

In his best New England Yankee voice, Mike repeated Benbow's question that morning, "Are you the owna' of this dina'?"

The owner glanced at his friends in the diner for a moment, then he answered, "Yes, I'm the owna'."

Benbow said, "Raise your own chickens, do ya?"

The owner said, "Yep... raise my own chickens alright."

Benbow said, "Bet you don't have any roosters, do ya?"

The owner said, "Don't need roosters — roosters don't lay eggs."

Benbow slid the money for his bill under the plate, then stood up and put on his coat. As he started to button his coat, Benbow said, "Need to get ya some roosters."

The owner said, "What makes ya think I need roosters?"

Benbow finished buttoning his coat and slipped on his hat. Then, just before going out the door, he said, "Cause... skunks been screwin' your chickens!"

They say that the second lap of a four-lap mile is the toughest — you're already a little tired, and you know you have 2 more laps to run after you finish this one. That's a fairly good description of the sentiments you will find on any crew bus that is carrying a crew out to a C-5 to fly a local training mission.

The crew reports for their briefing 3 hours and 15 minutes before they takeoff (to fly for 4 hours), so the guys usually feel like they're half beat before they ever reach the plane.

Mike always had a way of jazzing up that ride to airplane. I remember one cold morning when 7 or 8 of us were making that trip to the ship, and Mike decided to convert all of our long faces to smiles with a story about his most recent airline trip (Mike flew for TWA).

Mike told us that they landed their L-1011 in Athens, Greece, just as the sun was setting. They didn't have to leave until late the following evening, so Mike and the flight engineer, Bob, decided to visit the bar.

About half way through their second drink, a local lady named Athena decided to join them. It didn't take long for Mike to figure out that she had taken quite a liking to young Bob.

The bar closed relatively early, and Athena invited them over to her apartment for coffee. By this point Mike was feeling like the proverbial third wheel, so he excused himself. That was the last Mike saw of Bob until their report time the following evening.

They were so busy preparing for the flight back to the United States the following evening, that Mike didn't get a chance to query Bob about the remainder of his evening with Athena, until they were almost half way across the Atlantic.

Somewhere around 30° west, when Mike finally got around to mentioning Athena, Bob said, "Oh gosh, I don't even want to think about her." He shook his head slowly while he said, "It wasn't pretty."

Mike said, "What happened?"

Bob said, "Well, you know that foot odor problem I have?"

Mike said, "Yea."

They had flown together before, and it was common knowledge

that if Bob removed his shoes in the cockpit, everyone would immediately don their oxygen masks.

Bob said, "Well, I didn't change my socks or shoes before we went down to the bar last night. I knew that if Athena and I really started hitting it off — that the whole thing would come to a screeching halt the moment I took off my shoes.

"So, when we got to her apartment, I asked her if I could use her bathroom while she fixed the coffee. She said, 'Sure,' so I went in there and took off my socks and hid them under a bunch of toilet paper in the trash can.

"Then, I stuck my feet up in the sink and washed them real good. I knew she could hear me running the water in there and falling against the walls — I nearly broke my neck trying to stand on one foot and wash the other one in the sink — but I also knew that if I didn't get rid of that foot odor, that our date would be over.

"Anyway, I used a washcloth to wipe out the inside of my shoes and then dried them with a towel, then I dried off my feet and put my shoes back on, barefooted.

"When I went back to her living room, she set the coffee on the coffee table — then she said, 'I'll be right back,' and she went into the bathroom."

Bob looked at Mike and said, "Did you notice anything funny about her breath last night Mike?"

Mike said, "No, I didn't — but then I was never as close to her as you were, and the bar was pretty smoky."

Bob said, "That's what I figured out later — a couple of times I thought I might have smelled something like bad breath coming from her, but all that smoke and the drinks must have covered it up pretty well while we were in the bar."

Mike said, "Did she have halitosis?"

Bob said, "She must have — that or some other type of breath odor disease, because her breath smelled horrible."

Mike said, "Is that why she left you with the coffee and went into the bathroom."

Bob said, "It must have been, although I didn't realize it at the time. I heard her gargling and brushing and the water running like she was rinsing her mouth — but I'll tell you Mike, 10 minutes after she came out of that bathroom, her breath smelled like a badger's hind end."

Mike said, "What did you do?"

Bob said, "Well, after she came out of the bathroom we sat around and drank coffee and talked for awhile, and then she said, 'Bob, there's something I want to tell you.'

"I said, 'That's alright... I already know.'

"She said, 'What?'

"I said, 'You don't have to tell me — I already know.'

"She frowned for a few seconds, then she said, 'Exactly what is it that you think I don't have to tell you, because you already know?'

"I looked her straight in the eye and said, 'You ate my socks, didn't you?'"

Yea, having Mike along on the crew bus made the ride to the airplane much more enjoyable.

Out of the Mouths of Babes

I was surprised at the number of people forwarded copies of that anonymous little boy's letter to me, in which he described why he wanted to be an airline pilot. Since almost everyone who has been around aviation for a little while has already read the letter, we decided not to reprint it here. (If you haven't seen the letter yet, don't worry — you will soon. Half the cutups in the airline industry carry a xerox copy of it in their bag).

The letter's popularity does emphasize just how interesting it is to read about kids and what they think about flying. So, I thought I would start devoting one story in each book to that subject.

A fellow in Colorado Springs named Dale May sent me a story about a grade school teacher who asked her class some aviation questions. I enjoyed the answers so much, that I decided to copy the idea. (I know a good joke when I steal it). In Dale's story, the teacher asked her class, "Who are the three most important crew members on an airplane?"

One little boy answered, "The pilot, the navigator, and the percolator."

The teacher went on to ask, "Which crew member is the most important, and why?"

The same little boy answered, "The navigator is the most important, because he tells the pilot where to fly. He does this by determining the latitude and the longitude. The latitude tells him where he is, and the longitude tells him how long he can stay there."

Well, it just so happens that my daughter is attending the third grade at Braun Station elementary school in San Antonio, and her beautiful young teacher, Mrs. Modarelli, was kind enough to go along with my request to administer a similar test to her class. The following is a sampling of some of the answers these *third graders* offered to our test questions. (We didn't correct their spelling).

We started off with a simple warm-up question: **"What is the most important thing to remember about flying?"**

Our flight attendants will be relieved to learn that over 90% of the answers included some variation of the theme, "Bucal, your setbelt, and keep it bukled."

One little girl who apparently enjoys an enriched-sugar diet answered, "Not to freak out in the middle of the flight." (True, that is important).

Questions 2 and 3 asked, **"What does an airline captain do,"** and **"What does the copilot do?"**

A few of the answers:

"The captain tells what city *or state* there going to, and the copilot flys the plane."

"The captain flies the plane, and the copilot flies the plane when the captain is tired."

"The captain is a perfeshenol at crash landings, and the copilot is lerning to be a perfeshonl crash lander." (This is from the same little boy who thought air traffic controllers' duties included, "Helps the pilots crash land the planes." Come on kid—*all* of the landings aren't that bad).

My favorite answers to these questions came from the little girl whose father flies F-16s for the Guard at Kelly. She answered, "The captain flies the jet, and the copilot checks if anyone is on there tail." (Little Ms. fighter pilot, circa 2005).

The next couple of questions asked, **"Why do flight attendants fly on planes,"** and **"How do pilots learn how to fly?"**

The answers were pretty much what you would expect. It was touching if you knew the personal family history of some of the kids, and read that they thought the flight attendants were there to, "Help the children that have to fly alone."

Most of the kids said that pilots learn to fly, "On a pretend plane." (That's right, isn't it?)

The next question produced the most diverse range of answers, **"Where do flight attendants come from?"**

Several kids answered, "Earth," which is certainly correct in most cases, although one little boy did write, "The moon," which might also arguably be true in a few instances.

In a mild case of occupational dyslexia, one little boy wrote, "Flight attendants come from the Air Force, and pilots come from special schools."

It was interesting to observe the range of perspectives in their answers — several kids said that flight attendants came from, "All over the world," while others narrowed it down progressively to, "The North," — "Mississippi" (a great place to store them until you need them) — "Humen beans" — and "There mom's stomack." (That's pretty close, isn't it?)

The next question asked, **"What is the best thing and the worst thing about flying?"**

Most of the kids mentioned the fun of going places as the best part of flying, and the great majority cited the possibility of a crash as the worst part. I think one little girl might have brought some personal experiences to bear in her answer when she wrote, "The worst part is when you spill your soda all over your mommy's dress and throw up on her while she is cleaning up the mess. The best part is when you land, becauz it's over."

The next question asked, **"How do pilots know where they are?"**

The answers included, "They watch streets," — "They watch radars," — "They use a compus," — and "The air traffic controller tells them."

That question lead into the next one, which asked, **"What do air traffic controllers do?"**

Most of the kids had a pretty good grasp of controller's real duties, although I liked the way one little girl described it when she wrote, "They watch the road."

This question produced the longest answer on the test — it came from the lawyer's kid, who wrote a multi-sentence description of his theory of air traffic control. Essentially, he supposed that the controller thought up different ways of getting the airplane to its destination, which he then radioed to the copilot. The copilot was responsible for recording the controller's recommendations, and forwarding them to the captain. The captain would then mull over the various recommendations, and decide which one would work best.

The copilot would radio the captain's preferences back to the controller, who could either agree with the captain's decision, or attempt to persuade him to change his mind. He pretty much had their roles broken down to their basic components, with the controller as the "idea originator," the copilot as the "communicator," and the captain as the "master-debater."

The last question on the test asked, **"Would you rather be a pilot or a flight attendant? Why?"**

There were twice as many kids who said they wanted to be pilots as there were who wanted to be flight attendants, but only two of them offered an explanation as to why. One little boy (known for his clumsiness) wrote, "Pilots don't haf to walk aroun in the air and fall over," while the other scribbled, "Pilot, you get to were a hat."

Of the kids who said they preferred to be flight attendants, their answers to the "why?" part of the question included, "So I don't know when we are going to crash," — "because I wouldn't have to learn how to fly a plane," — and "becase its easy and you get to eat a lot."

One little girl wrote, "I don't know. A flight attendant I guess, becauz there is less disisions."

This last question also produced my favorite answer on the entire test. It was written by sweet little Heather, who neatly printed very sensible answers to all of the questions, and answered the last one with, "Flight attendant, because I would like to make people happy."

The Perils of Per Diem

I know what you're thinking, that you're going to read some story about a bunch of military pilots standing around at a party, with the TAC guys shooting their watches, the MAC guys talking about crew rests, and the SAC guys spilling their drinks.

Somewhere around the end of the story, one of the wives is going to break away from the other wives and storm over to her husband. The room will grow quiet at her menacing approach, and everyone will hear her demand, "Alright BOB—why haven't you ever mentioned this *per diem pay!?*"

Actually, the story I wanted to tell is just as classic, but I've never read it anywhere, so I thought it was about time we put it down on paper. There are two popular versions of this story. The airline version uses a doctor, lawyer, and airline captain as its characters. The military version uses the commanders of SAC (Strategic Air Command), TAC (Tactical Air Command), and MAC (Military Airlift Command) as its players.

I enjoy the esoteric rhymes which occur when I verbally tell the CINCSAC, TAC, and MAC version, so that's the rendition I'll use in this story. If you've never been in the Air Force, you will enjoy the yarn more if you remember that CINCSAC (Commander-In-Chief Strategic Air Command) is in charge of the the bomber, tanker, and strategic reconnaissance crews, who pull Alpha and Bravo alert duties. CINCTAC is responsible for the fighter guys, and CINCMAC answers for the cargo haulers.

The story goes that CINCSAC, CINCTAC, and CINCMAC all happen to be in Washington one weekend, and they get into a conversation about bird hunting. All three commanders are avid bird hunters, and of course each one believes that he owns the finest bird dog in the country.

CINCMAC is particularly adamant about the quality of his dog, which he suspects is a cross between a pit bull and a collie. (The type of dog that will chew your arm off and then go for help).

The conversation bounces back and forth between the escalating boasts of the commanders, until they finally agree to settle the question (of who has the best dog) with a little hunting trip to the eastern shore of the Chesapeake.

The following morning, CINCTAC tied their boat to the blind's pillars while CINCMAC and CINCSAC carried their gear up into the blind. CINCSAC was exceptionally eager to demonstrate the hunting

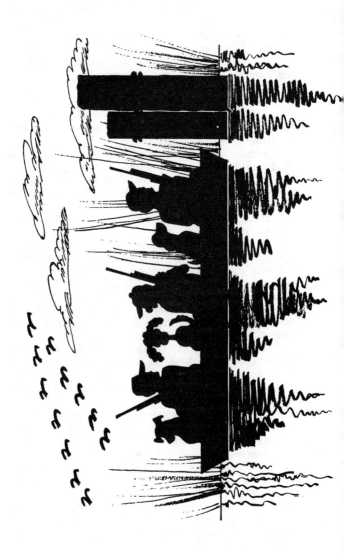

prowess of his dog, Alpha Bravo. So, CINCTAC and CINCMAC agreed to allow CINCSAC to shoot at the first ducks that approached their blind.

They didn't have to wait long before a pair of ducks flew within range. CINCSAC quickly dispatched both of them with his over-and-under Browning.

As soon as the second shot was off, CINCSAC ordered, "Get 'em Alpha Bravo," and the dog was in the water before the second duck hit the surface. Alpha Bravo swam straight to the first bird and retrieved it, gently placing it at the feet of CINCSAC, then he dove back into the icy water and quickly retrieved the second bird. Alpha Bravo's mouth was so gentle, that the birds' feathers were scarcely creased. When he lay the second bird (perfectly aligned with the first) at CINCSAC's feet, the other two commanders had to compliment CINCSAC on his outstanding animal.

Soon 4 more ducks approached the blind, but this time CINCTAC swung his automatic shotgun up and fired all 5 shots from the hip before CINCMAC or CINCSAC could respond. Two of the ducks fell into the Chesapeake, while the survivors quickly dove out of range.

CINCTAC ordered, "Get 'em Afterburner," and his dog dove out of the blind, performing a perfect swan dive. When he came up to the surface, Afterburner swam straight to the first duck, retrieved it, then kept going to the second bird and fit it into his mouth also. When Afterburner reentered the blind, he went straight to CINCTAC's game bag, pawed open the flap, and gently placed both birds inside. Afterburner nudged the flap closed with his nose then lay down at CINCTAC's feet.

Even the unflappable CINCSAC was impressed with Afterburner's performance, and he quickly said so. CINCMAC was just about to pay his compliments, when a racing pair of ducks swooped over the blind.

CINCMAC hadn't noticed the birds earlier since they approached from the rear of the blind, but he was determined to make up for the late target detection. He squeezed off the first round in his borrowed side-by-side shotgun while he was still raising the barrel, and the bird shot blew a 6-inch hole through the bottom of their boat.

Using his best tennis follow-through, CINCMAC kept the barrels swinging up as the ducks zoom-climbed away from the blind. If the blind's wooden window frame and camouflaging grass hadn't slowed down his bird shot so much, that round undoubtedly would have brought down the duck leader.

Temporarily confused by the swirl of wood chips, cordite, and grass pieces floating in the air inside the blind, CINCMAC ordered, "Get 'em Per Diem!"

During the ensuing confusion, Per Diem managed to eat all four birds and make love to the other two dogs — then he declared crew rest.

No wonder they say, "It's a dog's world."

It Was A Dark And Stormy Night

A pilot rarely has just one problem. Now, that's not to say that all problems are equal. Rather, one source problem, is usually causing several others. A good pilot can identify his source problem, fix it, and thus dispense with a whole slew of subsequent difficulties.

But, identifying that source problem isn't always as easy as it sounds. At least, that was the case a few weeks back when a reservist buddy of mine, Marshall Lessman, came storming into the pilot section, ranting and raving about the check ride he had taken from an active duty flight examiner at Altus AFB, Oklahoma.

Actually, Marshall's entrance interrupted a good story that Rich Terry was telling about watching old western movies on late night TV.

Rich was saying, "Did you ever notice that all of those old westerns are exactly alike? There's always a group of good cowboys who wear white, and a bad group of cowboys who wear black.

"The good cowboys could always whip up on the bad cowboys anytime they wanted to, but they're always saddled with the extra responsibility of some women and kids. Or, if the kids aren't there yet, then the women are pregnant, and about to give birth to the kids — usually right in the middle of some desert.

"How many times have you heard the leader of the good cowboys say, 'Partners, Mary Beth is about to have a baby, so here's what we have to do. Slim, you go find us a big bunch of clean rags. Red, you go round up all the soap you can find. Cooky, you gather up some firewood and start boiling buckets of water.'

"The cowpokes will nod earnestly and then start scampering off to fulfill their assigned duties, then one of them will turn around and say, 'Jake, is Mary Beth gonna have the baby right out here in the desert?'

"How many times have you ached for old Jake to tell him, "Why heck no Cooky — we're gonna wash the truck and take her to town!"

Rich obviously had more to say, but Marshall's irate entrance assured that we would never hear it.

We listened to Marshall chastise "Big Mac" and all that it entailed for awhile (Marshall had originally been a C-130 driver, so he was rightfully upset about the unit's transition to C-5s) but the group finally reached its "bitchin" saturation point.

So, I suggested that Marshall and I take a walk down to the stan/eval shop (Standardization & Evaluations), and discuss the matter with Rick Benbow, who happened to be heading up stan/eval at the time.

Marshall and I strolled down the hallway to Rick's office, where I explained the purpose of our visit to Rick. Rick proceeded to patiently listen to Marshall's allegations.

After about 20 minutes, Rick interrupted Marshall to ask, "Excuse me for just a moment Marshall. I think I know where you're going with these allegations of non-reservist prejudice on the part of your check pilot, but I happen to know the colonel who gave you that check ride, Colonel Snare.

"Now, when I worked with Snare, he seemed like a pretty good guy. So when I heard that you had experienced some problems with him, I made a call to Altus to see what really happened. So let me ask you this — do you think the fact that you stood on the bar in the Altus officer's club and described the C-5 as, 'two million rivets and five dozen turds flying close formation' had anything to do with your check ride grade?"

Marshall glared at Rick for a moment, then barked, "I'm entitled to my opinion."

Rick nodded and said, "What about that little incident when you set the bar on fire?"

Marshall said, "That wasn't my fault! Some jerk in the bar heard what I said about the C-5, and saw the C-130 patch on my sleeve, then said that the same thing could be said about a C-130!"

Rick said, "Uh-huh..?"

Marshall continued, "I was just waving my hands around while I told him that he was crazy, and I accidentally spilled whatever kind of flaming drink he was about to guzzle, and it ran all over the bar."

Rick said, "I see — what about the little incident where you poured beer all over the wing commander?"

Marshall said, "That was innocent enough, I was just trying to put out the fire spreading over the bar from that jerk's spilled drink! I grabbed the beer tap and started spraying the bar with it, and some of the beer spilled on that colonel."

Rick said, "Some of the beer?"

Marshall said, "Alright, a lot of the beer — but I was doing it for his protection. At first the beer just washed the burning drink over the edge of the bar and into the colonel's lap — so I had to spray him down to put out the fire!"

Rick said, "I see. What about the speeding ticket?"

Marshall said, "Yea, what a set up that was! That colonel was pretty hot after I watered him down with the beer keg, so I figured I had better hot-foot it off the base as quick as I could. I jumped in my rental car and started driving toward the front gate, and a cop stopped me and wrote up a speeding ticket for doing fifty-**SIX** miles per hour."

Rick said, "No kidding — it was a 55 miles per hour zone?"

Marshall said, "Well no, actually it was a 25 miles per hour zone."

Rick nodded thoughtfully for a moment, then he turned to Marshall and said, "Have you ever heard that story about the two old pirate buddies who run into each other at their pirate class reunion?"

Marshall shook his head, so Rick leaned back in his chair and related his version of "the pirate parable."

It seems that these two pirates were best friends throughout the pirate school that they attended on a Caribbean island, but after school they couldn't agree on which area of the world held the most promise for pirates at that time. So, they separated, and one spent the next 20 years in the Atlantic and Mediterranean, while the other spent his 20 years in the Pacific.

Both salty captains made a point of attending the class reunion. They were enjoying a mug of grog together after the first day's activities, when the Atlantic pirate said, "Say Henry, I see that you're wearing a wooden log."

Henry said, "Aye Constantine, it's a peg leg I've earned all right."

Constantine said, "I'll bet that's a good story — how *did* you earn that peg leg Henry?"

Henry said, "Well, it was a dark and stormy night. I always made my sailors tie themselves off to the ship whenever they were on deck in a storm, but I neglected the practice myself.

"I was working my way to the stern of the ship, when a wave washed over the deck unexpectedly, and carried me away. While I was trying to swim back to my ship, a shark bit off my right leg, just below the knee."

Constantine said, "Well blow down my rigging — a shark attack! That's quite a story Henry. But say me old ship mate, I see that you're sporting a hook on your right arm."

Henry guzzled a huge swallow of grog, then said, "Aye Constantine, lost me right hand at sea, so I wear this hook now. It works fine, just fine."

Constantine said, "Lost your hand at sea did you? How did it happen mate — a cutlass duel?"

Henry said, "Nay mate, it's not a cutlass wound. No, it was a dark and stormy night. I was trying to make my way across our icy deck in the North Pacific, when the ship struck ice and pitched to starboard. I couldn't keep my footing with peg leg, so I was tossed overboard.

"I tried to swim back to my ship, but I couldn't make good time

in the water with my peg leg. A killer whale made a pass at me just as I reached the ship, and I stretched out my right hand to fend him off. The devil fish took off my hand, just below the wrist."

Constantine said, "Incredible! First a shark attack, and then a killer whale! That surely would have killed a lesser man mate. But say, I notice that you're wearing an eye patch over your right eye."

Henry said, "Aye mate, lost my right eye at anchor off Hawaii, so I wear my black patch now with the skull and cross bones printed on it. Do you like it?"

Constantine said, "Aye mate — it gives you a salty, fiendish look. But, how did you lose your eye?"

Henry said, "Well mate, it was a bright and shiny day. I was enjoying the clouds floating over the ship and the sound of the breeze in the rigging, when I noticed a sea gull soaring overhead. I looked up to admire the flight of the bird, and damn if it didn't crap right in my eye."

Constantine shook his head and said, "That's really too bad Henry — I didn't even know that sea gull crap could put out an eye."

Henry said, "It can't you fool — it was the first day I wore my new hook!"

When Rick finished the story, Marshall didn't say anything. He looked at Rick for a few moments, then he just smiled and shook his head. Finally, he stood up and walked out of the office.

I asked Rick, "Think that did any good?"

Rick said, "I doubt it, but you never can tell. Maybe he'll tie himself off the next time he starts across a stormy deck."

I hope so, I'm fairly fond of Marshall.

Red Eye Blues

It's difficult for most airline pilots to find the fun in riding around in an airplane all night, then landing just as the sun comes up. But, red eyes are part of the job. So, everyone learns to just hope for a good crew, and try to make the most of it.

Sig Christenson was my captain on the last red eye I flew. We also had a delightful young flight attendant on the crew named Lynn Vely. Sometime around 2 am, it seemed like the coffee just wouldn't keep us awake any more, so we started telling stories to make sure we didn't nod off.

Earlier in the trip, Sig mentioned that he had just finished annual refresher training, so I asked, "Did everything go okay in the simulator this year?"

Sig said, "Gosh, I'll tell you — they threw too many emergencies at me this year. When I got back to my hotel room from the simulator checkride, the phone rang, and I immediately silenced the bell."

I said, "Which check pilot did you have this year?"

Sig chuckled then said, "I drew old Charlie Smith this year — do you know Charlie?"

I shook my head, "No," so Sig decided to keep us awake for awhile by telling Lynn and I all about Charlie Smith.

Sig said, "Charlie just finalized his fourth divorce. Everyone has been telling him for years that it would be a lot cheaper for him to stay single, and just go out and find some woman that he hated every 7 or 8 years — and buy her a house.

"But, Charlie has always been real big on having kids, and he felt like the only realistic way to go about that was to get married.

"Unfortunately, not one of his 4 wives produced any children for him. It was really starting to bother Charlie that he was growing old, and he hadn't reproduced himself. It didn't bother him enough to risk getting married again though, he knew he couldn't afford that.

"So, Charlie did some research, and he found out all there was to know about the sperm banks that they have on the west coast.

"Charlie decided that one of these "depositories" in Los Angeles was exactly the vehicle he was searching for, so he went through their lengthy application process, and finally qualified as a donor.

"He said that he was pretty nervous on the day that he flew out there to make his deposit, but the facility had a very nice young lady who processed his paperwork and made him feel like he was dealing with professionals.

"He must have still appeared a little uneasy though when the time actually came to take his little bottle and his Playboy magazine down to the "donor room" — because he said that the lady made a point of telling him, 'Just take all the time you need.'

"Apparently Charlie finally maxed out their patience. He said that after about 3 hours in the donor room, the lady finally knocked on the door and asked, 'Mr. Smith, are you all right... do you need any help?'

"Charlie said that he opened the door and looked her right in the eye and said, 'As a matter of fact, I do need some assistance. I've beat and beat and beat on this thing — I've twisted it and pounded it — I've even beat it against the side of the easy chair... but I just can't get the lid off this damn bottle."

I got a kick out the story, but Lynn said, "Ok, if we're going to tell them that bad, I have a frog joke for you."

Lynn went on to tell the story about Polly Black, the bank's loan officer, who was busily working at her desk one day when she heard a "Plop, plop, plop."

Polly looked up just in time to see a frog hopping up onto the chair beside her desk.

Polly was a little startled at first, but the frog was dressed nicely and seemed to be waiting for her attention, so she finally said, "Can I help you?"

The frog said, "Yes, you can. I would like to apply for a loan."

The frog went on to explain why he needed the money, and how much he wanted to borrow. Polly discussed the applicable interest rates and repayment schedules with the frog.

Finally, Polly asked, "What collateral can you provide to secure this loan?"

The frog shrugged his little green shoulders and said, "The only thing I have that might suffice as collateral is a grandfather's clock that my uncle left to me."

Polly said, "Gosh, I really don't know if that will work or not. I'll tell you what, you wait here, and I'll talk to my supervisor about this and see what he thinks."

The frog waited patiently while Polly walked to her supervisor's office and discussed the matter with him. When she returned, she told the frog, "Mr. Mooney will be out any minute with an answer — he just has to check the bank's list of acceptable collateral items to see if your frog-sized grandfather's clock falls under any of the categories."

A few moments later, Mr. Mooney emerged from his office, carrying a large book with a place marker sticking out from between it's pages.

Polly Black said, "Well?"

Mr. Mooney shrugged his shoulders and said, "It's a knick knack Polly Black, give the frog a loan."

It was Sig's turn to pull Lynn's chain, he asked her, "Was Polly Black pretty? You could have jazzed that story up a lot by making Polly an ex-Playboy bunny you know."

Lynn was frowning, so Sig kept it up, "I like stories about beautiful women while I'm out on the road. I suppose it's because I get lonely sometimes. I was watching TV last night and thinking, 'You know, that Wilma Flintstone doesn't have a bad body. She's no Judy Jetson mind you, but she's not bad at all.'"

Lynn's frown wasn't letting up, so Sig said, "Ok, I'm sorry. The only time I open my mouth anymore is to change feet."

That got Lynn to smile again, so Sig said, "I'm not as bad as some of my friends. I have a friend at Eastern who has a habit of saying exactly the wrong thing at exactly the wrong time."

Sig gave us several examples of his Eastern buddy's screw ups, but my favorite was his story about his friend walking through the terminal at La Guardia on Christmas eve.

Sig's buddy is a captain, and Sig claimed that if I printed his name, every Eastern pilot on the seniority list prior to 1989 would know who I was talking about. A couple of years ago this captain was walking through the terminal with his first officer, and they just happened to be passing by the ticket counter when a Brinks armored car arrived to pick up the ticket counter's cash.

Well, you can imagine that New York terminal on Christmas eve — wall to wall people, with everyone trying to push and shove their way through the teeming masses to their personal destinations.

This captain was strolling along with his suitcase and pubs bag, just sort of lost in his own little world, when all at once he came face to face with a Brinks armored truck guard, in uniform, who was trying to make his way to the ticket counter.

The captain looked down at the guard's waist, and all he could see was the big revolver sticking out of the guard's holster. An astonished look appeared on the guard's face when the captain's booming voice suddenly resonated throughout the terminal... **"HE'S GOT A GUN! HE'S GOT A GUN!"**

Instantly, pandemonium reigned. People started diving off

escalators, jumping behind ticket counters, and diving through the baggage conveyor belt doors — and all the while the Brinks guard just stood there, dumbfounded.

The first officer realized what was going on, so he dropped his bags and grabbed the captain. He had to shout to make himself heard over all the screaming passengers, but he finally managed to make the captain realize that, "It's okay — he's *supposed* to have a gun — he's a *guard!*"

Amazingly, instead of just wandering off and disappearing, the captain started walking through the terminal, shouting, "It's okay folks, you can come out now. He's just a guard. He's *supposed* to have a gun. You can come out now."

Lynn told us the story that was going around at that time about the airline captain who gets killed in a car wreck with Paul Newman and Robert Redford.

When the three of them get to heaven, St. Peter tells Paul Newman, "Paul Newman, because of your transgressions on Earth, you will spend eternity with the person you select by opening one of three doors."

St. Peter pointed at three doors behind him and said, "Select a door now."

Paul Newman selected door number one, and the lady who stepped out when the door opened was, to put it kindly, not someone you would want to spend eternity with. Paul Newman shuddered for a minute, then he and his new mate strolled away together.

St. Peter turned to Robert Redford and said, "Robert Redford, because of your transgressions on Earth, you will spend eternity with the person you select by opening one of the remaining doors."

Robert Redford selected door number two, and if he could have, he undoubtedly would have swapped his new mate for the one Paul Newman ended up with. After a moment of mental preparations, however, Robert Redford and his new mate wandered away together.

The airline captain was pretty concerned by now, having seen the way things were going. But, to his surprise, St. Peter did not ask him to select the only remaining door. Instead, St. Peter walked back and opened the door himself, and out walked Bo Derick.

St. Peter turned to Bo and said, "Bo Derick, because of your transgressions on Earth..."

Sig said, "Did you say they used an elevator to get to heaven?"
Lynn said, "I didn't say."
Sig said, "Too bad — I have a good elevator story I could append

to that."

We told Sig it was okay to tell it anyway, so he told us the tale about an elderly couple from rural Pennsylvania, who finally decided to take a trip out of the state. The lady, Ethel, was 60 years old, and she had never traveled outside of of Pennsylvania. As a matter of fact, she had only been to the closest city, Pittsburgh, twice in her life.

Ethel's husband, Raymond, had traveled a little bit more, but he couldn't convince Ethel to leave the house to travel with him. She was much too afraid of becoming the victim of some heinous crime.

Ethel and Raymond were good friends with another retired couple, however, who were avid travelers. When US Air started their Las Vegas service, these two retired jet-setters immediately went to the city of lights, where of course they had a great time.

When they returned, they kept talking about Las Vegas. They talked about their trip so much, that Raymond finally decided that he just had to go. The three of them worked on Ethel for weeks, telling her how cheap the trip would be if they went on a senior citizen discount fare and booked their flights and rooms in advance, and how safe it would be, and how much fun they would have.

Finally, when Ethel realized that Raymond intended to go with or without her, she conceded to accompany them to (in her words) the "city of sin."

Everything went fine during their flight and the taxi ride from the airport to the cassino where they were staying, but Ethel clung to Raymond's arm continually, lest someone drag her away and rob her. This went on for the first couple of days, but finally, after watching some good shows and enjoying the excellent food, Ethel started to loosen up a little bit.

Then, it happened. They were waiting in line to get into a show, and Ethel decided to drop a coin into one of the slot machines lining the walls of the waiting area. She was instantly hooked. As soon as the show was over, Ethel was right back on the floor of the cassino, feeding the one-armed bandits.

Raymond couldn't drag her away from the machines, and it finally started to get late. Their traveling companions had already retired.

Raymond begged Ethel to stop for the evening, but she insisted that she was on too much of a roll to stop. Raymond asked her if she could find her way upstairs to their room by herself. She reacted huffily — insulted that he would even insinuate that she couldn't. Raymond said, "Fine, I'm going to stop off at our friends' room and tell them goodnight, and I'll see you in our room in a little while then."

Ethel waved her hand and said, "Yea, sure, see you later," but her eyes never left the spinning wheels in front of her.

Raymond shook his head and walked away to the elevators, and Ethel continued to drop quarters into the machine, until all at once she hit 3 lucky sevens in a row!

Lights started flashing, bells rang and horns blew, and then the slot machine started spitting out quarters — one hundred dollars' worth! Ethel couldn't believe it — she hurriedly gathered up more cardboard tubs and held them under the machine to collect the quarters.

When the machine finally stopped coughing out quarters, Ethel had 6 tubs full, and quite a crowd staring at her. In all the excitement of collecting the coins, she hadn't noticed the crowd gathering to enjoy her antics. All the paranoia she had originally felt about going to Las Vegas, returned.

She was certain that someone in the crowd intended to knock her on the head and take her new found fortune. When a cassino employee offered to help her trade in the tubs of quarters for a check, she immediately waved him away with her cane. She had no intention of letting anyone get close to her quarters.

But, now she found herself in a dilemma. How to get the quarters up to her room? She stacked the heavy tubs of coins on top of each other, and managed to push them to a side wall next to a house phone. She tried to call her room, but there was no answer.

"Raymond must still be visiting with our friends," she thought.

She couldn't remember which room their friends were staying in, so there was only one thing to do. She would have to get the money to the room by herself.

Ethel shoved the tubs full of coins to the elevator, and pushed the up button. In a few moments the elevator door opened, and Ethel placed one of the tubs in the doorway to hold the door open while she loaded the other tubs inside. Unfortunately, a young couple walked past her tub and into the elevator, where they waited impatiently for her.

There was no way that Ethel was going to get into an elevator with other people, who could rob her and get away before she could summon help. So, Ethel removed her tub of quarters from the doorway and allowed the couple to go up.

The same process repeated itself twice more before Ethel was finally able to load all of her tubs into the elevator and close the door before anyone could join her. She pressed the button for the 11th floor, and leaned back against the wall, nearly exhausted.

The door closed and the elevator started up. Ethel was still holding the tub of quarters that she had used to hold the door open. She was about to put it down, when she suddenly noticed that the elevator was stopping!

To her horror, the elevator arrested its ascent, and when the door opened, Ethel found herself face to face with a tall, lanky black man holding a dog's leash. At the other end of the leash, was the biggest Doberman pincer that Ethel had ever seen.

The tall black man led the dog into the elevator and stood against the back wall. Before Ethel could think of any action to take, the door closed, and the elevator started to rise again.

Ethel was just about to press the button of the next floor to get the elevator to stop so she could get out, when she heard the black man command, *"Lie down!"*

CRASH! Quarters sprayed all over the floor of the elevator as Ethel dropped the tub and immediately spread eagled herself on the floor crying, "Please, don't hurt me!"

The shocked gentleman immediately said, "Oh gosh lady — please get up. I was yelling at this stupid dog! Please get up lady."

Ethel didn't know what to do at first, but when the black man knelt beside her and started gathering up her quarters and placing them back into the tub, she decided she could trust him. Then, she couldn't stop talking.

While the man retrieved her scattered coins, Ethel's mouth jabbered out syllables like a machine gun, "I won all this money and I wanted to get it to the room but Raymond couldn't help me because he didn't know I had won it and he was in our friends' room and I couldn't think of their number to call them and people kept getting on the elevator and I waited until I could ride alone and I used the quarters to hold the door open..."

The bewildered black man just kept shaking his head while he gathered up the coins and waited for the elevator to stop on Ethel's floor. When the door finally opened, the man said, "Look lady, these tubs are too heavy for you to carry. Why don't you let me carry them to your room? I'll set them down in the hallway right outside your door, and you can take them in after I've left. The dog will guard us while I carry them down there."

Ethel agreed, and soon the huffing black man found himself standing outside Ethel's door while she fumbled with her key, trying to unlock the room. Raymond heard the commotion, so he opened the door from inside the room.

When he looked past Ethel and saw the tall black man standing there with his arms full of coin tubs and an attack dog at his side, Raymond didn't know what to think. The gentleman quickly set the tubs down just inside the door, then said, "Sir, there was a little mix up in the elevator which I'm very sorry about. Anyway, here's your money, and I apologize."

Raymond couldn't fathom what he was talking about. Ethel said, "Thank you, and don't worry about the elevator, that's all right sonny."

The black man flashed an embarrassed smile and wiped the sweat from his forehead, then he took his dog and left.

Of course the next morning when they met their friends for breakfast, Ethel couldn't stop talking about her adventure. Their friends had a good laugh at the story and they educated her on the process of cashing in winnings for a check, then they returned to their rooms and packed their bags for the trip home.

When Raymond approached the checkout desk later in the morning, he was surprised to hear the clerk say, "Oh, so you're the people who were in room 1111. Your bill is already taken care of."

Raymond said, "What do you mean?"

The clerk said, "Apparently there was some sort of an incident with your wife in an elevator, and the gentleman involved was so embarrassed about it that he wanted to pay your room bill to try to make it up to you."

Raymond said, "Is that so?"

The clerk said, "Yes, it is. As a matter of fact, we informed him that you were traveling with friends, and he paid their room bill also."

Raymond said, "Do you mind if I have a look at the ticket?"

The desk clerk said, "Not at all, you can see it is signed on the bottom by the gentleman paying the bill."

Raymond examined the ticket for a moment, then said, "Just exactly who is this Lionel Ritchie fella anyway?"

Things were calm for a little while, then Sig asked Lynn if she had obtained a passport yet. Lynn said that she had, and asked Sig if he had one.

Sig answered, "Yea, I did get one, but in the process of getting my passport I found out when I am going to die."

I asked what he meant by that, and he told me, "Well, the post office wants to see your *birth certificate* before they will give you the passport paperwork. When I dug mine out, I noticed that the darn thing has an expiration date printed on it!"

Lynn said, "You just happened to notice that huh?," and Sig said,

"Yep, it just goes to show — you can observe a lot just by watching."

Lynn asked, "So you consider yourself to be a pretty observant guy, huh?"

Sig turned around so he could look at her and answered, "I think I do a lot better job of keeping up with what's going on than that yahoo on the Newlywed show the other night — did you see it?"

Lynn and I assured him that we didn't know what he was talking about, so Sig told us that now-classic story about the newlywed game. I still don't know whether it's a true story or not, but I have heard people say that they watched the episode the night that it happened.

Anyway, the story goes that the men returned to the stage, to see if they could match their brides' answers to the question, "Where was the most unusual place you ever made whoopee?"

The first couple drew a good chuckle from the audience when they matched with their answer, "In an elevator."

The gentleman in the second couple tried to hedge his answer a little bit at first, when he said, "In a car."

Bob Eubanks pressed him for a bit more specific answer, and he finally confessed, "Ok, it was a convertible, at a drive-in."

That drew a good laugh from the entire audience, but it was the last contestant who really slew them. After Bob put the same question to this gentleman, he rubbed his chin thoughtfully and looked at the ceiling for awhile, then finally said, "I think I'll have to go with the butt — in the butt Bob, in the butt."

Santa's Line Check

My class at US Air started training on June the 2nd, 1986. We had a great class. As a matter of fact, everybody got along so well, that we have a class reunion at least twice a year — usually Thanksgiving day and Christmas eve.

Everyone congregates down in the crew room for a little while, then we fill out our paperwork, round up our junior captains, and takeoff into the wild grey yonder. That's one of the great ironies about airline flying — on the busiest flying days of the year, the most-junior crews are out there doing all the flying.

The upside of the situation is that you get to see all your friends who have been flying senior first officer trips, but have recently upgraded to junior Captain slots. That was the case last Christmas eve, when I felt a hand on my shoulder and turned around to find my old friend, Jose Portela, standing there in his brand new captain's uniform.

Jose recently took a bid as a BAC-111 captain. I didn't get a chance to fly the BAC before US Air retired them, but most of my friends who did, told me it fell into that category of, "Things that are fun to do, but you don't want people to find out you did it."

Anyway, Jose was busy telling everyone this story called, Santa's Line Check.

It seems that one Christmas eve not too long ago, an FAA air carrier inspector showed up at Santa's house just about the time that Santa was getting ready to launch on his annual around-the-world flight. The FAA guy was carrying a long, grey, nylon ski bag.

When Santa answered the doorbell, the FAA examiner leaned his ski bag against the side of the house and said, "Good evening Mr. Claus. My name is Ed Garrard, and I was wondering if you might be flying south this evening."

Santa shook hands with Ed and said, "Ho ho ho — as a matter of fact, I was planning a flight south this evening."

Ed said, "Boy, that's great, because every flight out of the North Pole is overbooked tonight. I was up here doing a little skiing, but I wanted to get home to Dallas for Christmas tomorrow morning.

"When I found out all the flights were overbooked, I started to call home and tell the family I wasn't going to make it by tomorrow morning, and then I remembered that you normally have a flight going to Dallas tonight."

Santa said, "I sure do, every December 24th."

Ed said, "Great, I was wondering if I could catch a ride down there with you."

Santa said, "Well I don't know, I'm normally pretty full when I leave home."

Ed pulled his identification out of his wallet and said, "I see. Well Santa, as you can see, I'm an inspector for the FAA. I took the liberty of checking your record, and I couldn't find any record of your last standardization ride."

Santa said, "My what?"

Ed said, "Your standardization ride Santa. We're responsible for ensuring that everyone operating in US airspace operates under a standardized set of procedures."

Santa said, "What are you talking about? I'm the only Santa Claus — who am I going to be standardized with?"

Ed said, "That's not important Santa, the point is that nothing is more important than standardization."

Santa looked at Ed with less than a merry chuckle in his eye.

Ed said, "Look, maybe this will explain it to you. Did you ever hear the story about the entrepreneur who made his millions, and then went to India to seek the meaning of life?"

Santa shook his head.

Ed said, "Well, he spent hundreds of thousands of dollars to buy climbing equipment and supplies. Then, he paid porters to carry all of it to a base camp on a mountain. He intended to climb the mountain and ask the wise man who lived on its peak, 'What is the meaning of life?'

"His porters fell off the mountain with his supplies. He ran out of food, but he still climbed the mountain. He didn't have the proper equipment after his porters fell, but he still climbed with his bare hands until he reached the summit.

"When he finally crawled into the wise man's cave, he found him sitting in front of a fire, meditating. The entrepreneur said, 'Wise man, what is the answer?'

"The wise man opened his eyes and said, 'The answer is — standardization.'

"The entrepreneur said, 'Are you *crazy?* I spend hundreds of thousands of dollars, and lose all of my porters and equipment, but still climb to the top of this mountain on my hands and knees — and you have the *audacity* to tell me that the answer is, *Standardization!*'

"The wise man nodded slowly for a few moments, then finally said, 'Ok... so it's *not* standardization.'"

Santa eyed Ed coldly for a few moments, then said, "I don't see the point Ed."

Ed said, "The point is, that I need a ride to Dallas, and you need a checkride, so I'll be riding your jumpseat tonight."

Santa said, "I don't have time to argue with you. I don't think I actually require a no-notice checkride — but if you will just sit down in the back of the sleigh, be quiet, and not touch anything, I'll drop you off in Dallas."

Ed said, "You won't even know I'm there."

Ed watched while the elves finished loading Santa's sleigh and placed the reindeer in their harnesses. When they were finished, Santa emerged from his house and took his seat.

Santa glanced at Ed and said, "Are you coming or not?"

"Hum," Ed thought, "no preflight, no weight-and-balance computations, no flight plan, no flashlight, no flight publications — this is *horrible!*"

Ed stored his ski bag under his seat in the back of the sleigh then said, "All ready back here."

Rudolph illuminated his nose to signal he was ready, then Santa shouted, "On Dasher and Dancer and Prancer and Vixen, on Comet and Cupid and Donner and Blitzen," and the sleigh began a gentle climbing turn.

Ed thought, "No checklist either, huh?"

Santa heard a minor commotion in the back seat, so he turned around to see what it was. He was surprised to see Ed unzipping his ski bag. Instead of removing a set of skis or poles, however, Ed drew a 30.06 caliber deer rifle out of the bag and slid the bolt back to work a round into the chamber!

Ed stood up so he could fire over Santa's head, and took careful aim at the back of Cupid's head.

BLAM!

Ed lowered the rifle and said, "Ok you nonstandard old geezer — you just lost one on takeoff. Let's see you handle *that* without a checklist."

I wonder if Jose will be senior enough on the MD-80 this year to get Christmas off?

The Rabbit Died

Gary Saathoff is a good friend of mine who currently flies for Southwest Airlines. Gary is an "Aggie" (a graduate of Texas A & M University).

Gary came pretty close to not making it as an Aggie though — at one point he was nearly thrown out of the school for assassinating a parrot. That was when Gary thought he wanted to be a veterinarian instead of an airline pilot.

It happened innocently enough. A lady brought her pet parrot into the veterinarian section of the school to have a growth removed from his beak. Of course, Gary knew that the parrot wouldn't sit still while he burned the growth off with an electric hot-tip, so he anesthetized the bird.

That was easy enough, Gary just put the bird into a small cardboard box and squirted in a little ether. When the parrot stopped flopping around, he knew he was asleep.

The problem came, when Gary tried to burn off the growth without removing the bird from the box. The electricity arced from the hot-tip to the beak, and the spark ignited the ether fumes.

BLAMM!!!

They said it rained little yellow feathers for over 5 minutes.

Well, Gary convinced the heart-broken old lady that the whole thing was a complete accident, so she didn't press the matter and Gary made it through school — albeit with a new ambition to succeed as an airline pilot instead of as a veterinarian.

His problems with animals were far from over though, as Gary's neighbors can readily attest to. After he was hired by Southwest, Gary moved to Houston and spent several happy months sitting reserve for the airline.

Of course his new neighbors soon discovered that Gary spent a lot of time sitting around the house waiting for the phone to ring, so they began asking him to do little favors for them in between his mad dashes to the airport. Being the "good Samaritan" type person that he is, Gary was always happy to help his neighbors.

One of his neighbors, Bill Muellner, asked Gary to watch his house for him while Bill took his family on a vacation trip to Disney World. Everything went smoothly until the day before the Muellners were scheduled to return.

On that day, Gary glanced up from his newspaper and noticed that his dog Bad Eye, was playing with something in the backyard. He couldn't quite tell what Bad Eye's new toy was, so Gary went outside

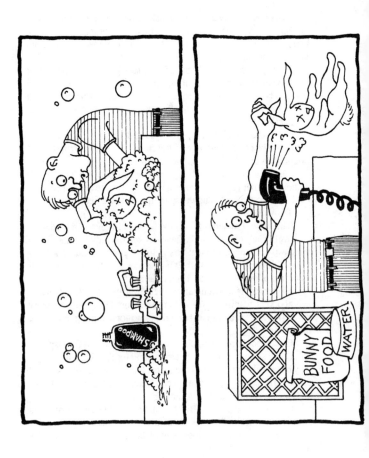

and called Bad Eye over to him.

Low and behold, there in Bad Eye's jaws — Gary recognized the carcass of the Muellners' pet rabbit!

A couple of good kicks and several loud yells later, Gary managed to convince Bad Eye to give up the dead bunny. The first thing that went through his mind, was how he could replace it.

Unfortunately, the white rabbit had several distinctive black and brown spots, which made it highly unlikely that Gary could find a replacement colored closely enough to the original to fool the Muellner children.

Gary was really feeling terrible about the incident by now. Bill had forgotten to mention the rabbit to him, so Gary hadn't fed or watered the pet during the week they had been away.

The thought of explaining to the Muellner children how their pet rabbit had met his doom after managing to escape his pen in search of food — well, it was just too much for Gary to bear.

When he examined the rabbit more closely, Gary noticed that Bad Eye hadn't actually chewed up the bunny too badly. The fur was dirty from being dragged around by Bad Eye, but there were only a couple of small puncture wounds, which could be easily hidden! Gary had an idea.

He took the rabbit inside to his bathroom, where he gave him a good shampoo and a blow-dry with his wife's hair dryer. Then, Gary returned the bunny to his pen behind the Muellners' house. He was careful to place a bowl of water and some food in the pen before he closed the door.

When the Muellners returned the following day, Gary waited until late in the afternoon before going over to visit them. He wanted them to have plenty of time to unpack their bags and look around the house before he talked to them.

Finally, Gary saw Bill watering his front lawn, and he knew that his chance had come.

Gary waved and smiled as he walked across the street and shouted, "Welcome back neighbor."

Bill waved back and shouted, "Hi Gary, it's good to be back."

They chatted about the vacation for a little while, then Gary said, "Was everything all right in the house when you went in?"

Bill said, "It sure was, thanks a million. We sure do appreciate you taking care of things for us."

Gary said, "No problem at all."

Bill said, "There was one thing that was pretty bizarre though..."

Gary said, "Really, what was that?"

Bill said, "Well, when the boys went out back to play, they found their pet rabbit lying in his pen — dead as a doornail. They said his little front paws were even crossed over his chest, as if he had gone peacefully in his sleep."

Gary said, "You don't say! Just up and died on you while yall were away on vacation, huh?"

Bill said, "No... that's the bizarre part. That rabbit died the day before we left on vacation. The boys and I buried him in the back yard before we left."

Yea, we always thought that old Gary made a good decision when he gave up his veterinarian plans for an airline career.

A Bunch of Bull

As I write this, I'm commuting home from one of the more interesting trips of my airline career — my last, for awhile at least, in the 737-200. Fortunately I had a great captain, Rob Johnson, and a fine group of flight attendants: Ken, Karen, and Susan. Ken is one of the regulars in the crash-pad I frequent in Pittsburgh.

We spent the first night of the trip in Toronto — we got in at 10 pm and didn't leave until 3:30 pm the next day. With all that time to kill, Ken wanted to go downtown for lunch, so he and I signed out the company car that we keep in Toronto and drove it from the Carlton Place hotel (close to the airport) all the way downtown to the Chinatown district.

We were careful to select a parking area where a lot of other cars were already parked (we were a little nervous about someone tampering with the car). We finally grabbed a parking space directly in front of a sign post. There was a sign on the lamp post which said:

> No Parking
> 3:30 to 6:30
> Mon - Fri

As it was noon on Sunday — we felt pretty good about leaving the car there. We strolled around Chinatown for awhile, gawking at all the sights and trying to decide on a restaurant for lunch. While we strolled through the open air markets, Ken told me the story about the Chinaman who applied for a job in a gold mine, along with a Texan and an Englishman.

The gold mine foreman said, "You're in luck, I can use all three of you."

The foreman pointed to the Texan and said, "A big strong guy like you ought to be good at digging, so I'll put you in charge of excavation."

He handed the Texan a shovel, then turned to the Englishman and said, "You look pretty wiry — I imagine you would hold up pretty well at hauling the dirt and gold out of the mine."

The foreman pointed toward a wheelbarrow and said, "I'm making you responsible for that wheelbarrow — you're in charge of evacuation."

While the Englishman walked away to retrieve the wheelbarrow, the foreman turned his attention to the Chinaman and said, "You're pretty small for hard labor — I think I'll put you in charge of supplies."

The Chinaman nodded eagerly and the foreman sent all three of them off toward the mine. A few hours later, he decided to check on their progress. About halfway down the shaft, he encountered the Englishman, pushing a load of dirt toward the mouth of the mine.

The foreman said, "Good, good — keep up the good work," then he continued toward the end of the shaft, where he found the Texan hard at work digging out the ore.

The foreman said, "You're doing great. You and that Englishman are really moving some ore."

The Texan said, "Thanks," without breaking stride. The foreman looked around a few moments, then said, "Say, you wouldn't know where that Chinaman is, would you?"

The Texan said, "The last time I saw him, he was walking down that closed shaft about a hundred yards back with a light and a pistol."

Of course that immediately piqued the foreman's curiosity, so he set out to find the missing Chinaman. The foreman walked back to the abandoned shaft and marched all the way to its end without encountering the Chinaman.

Just as he turned around to walk back to the main shaft, the Chinaman jumped out of his hiding place behind a huge rock and flipped on his flashlight with the beam pointed straight at the foreman's face. The next sound the foreman heard was, "BLAM! BLAM! BLAM! BLAM! BLAM! BLAM!," six reports from the Chinaman's pistol!

The startled foreman shined his light at the Chinaman's face, and the Chinaman shouted, **"Suplize! Suplize!"**

Ken and I found a good place to grab some egg-drop lobster soup, then we hustled back to the car. We were a little upset to discover that the company car (along with all the other cars parked along that street) had been towed away! I ran down a tow-truck driver that I noticed on a side street, and when I asked him what happened to the cars along the main avenue, he said, "We towed them to 10 York street, ay?"

Gosh, welcome to my nightmare. We couldn't find a taxi to take us to the impound lot, nor any cops, and none of the tow-truck drivers would give us a lift. We were rapidly running out of time. To the Torontoans' credit, we *were* saved by a city bus driver who heard me arguing with the tow-truck driver in the middle of the street, and realized our plight.

The bus driver waved us onto his bus and drove off his normal route to deliver us to the impound lot as quickly as possible. He didn't even charge us for the lift.

With launch time rapidly approaching, we contemplated trying to steal back the car — but they had it locked up on the back of the lot. So, I ran into the "Stick-em-up" building and paid $81 to get the car back. The folks taking the money at the impound lot were in no mood to listen to complaints, so our only alternative was to pay and run.

My only comment to the Toronto parking authorities is, "It's pretty damned easy to steal cars when you have a badge and a gun, ay?"

Anyway, I called Rob from the impound lot and told him we were buying back the car, and we would be a little late for the bus. He couldn't have been more cool about the situation — he offered to help anyway he could from the hotel. When I told him there was nothing he could do, he said to just make it to the plane as fast as we could and he, Karen, and Susan would get everything ready.

Well, we made an on-time takeoff out of Toronto, and Ken and I spent the next few hours trying to get our heart rate back to normal (Ken is on probation!). When we finally arrived in Providence that night, Rob and I got another chance to enjoy our favorite pastime while waiting for the hotel van. We call it, "Let's see how hard we can make the girls laugh."

Fortunately, Rob read my first book, so we were able to play off the same sheet of music most of the time, which is a big help when you're trying to play straight-man for one another. We got Susan and Karen going pretty good with our rendition of, The Old Bull and the Young Bull (see book 1) but it was the follow-on story (which Rob told) that really slew them.

Rob said, "As long as we're talking about bulls, did you hear the one about the 3 bulls standing in the pasture, talking about the new bull that was supposed to be coming to the ranch?"

I gave him a pretty good straight-man "come-on," so Rob said, "Well, the biggest and oldest bull said, 'I don't know what kind of bull they're bringing in here, but he had sure better stay away from my 20 cows.'

"The medium-sized bull said, 'You got that right. I don't care who he is, if he comes around any of my 10 cows, I'll teach him how we do business on this ranch.'

"The youngest and smallest bull said, 'You guys said it. If this new guy comes within 20 feet of one of my 5 cows, I'll take him downtown.'

"About that time an enormous tractor-trailer truck pulled up just on the other side of the fence, and the driver got out and let down the

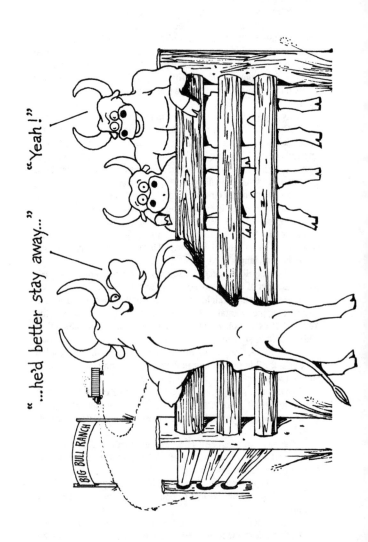

back ramp. All 3 bulls were stunned when they saw the size of the bull that started backing down the ramp. His back was so tall that he had to duck his head when his front legs came to the edge of the ramp.

"The oldest bull said, 'You know, I've been thinking about slacking off a little bit. I've been awful busy around here for a long time, and I was thinking that maybe if I could find someone else to take care of, say 10 of my cows, that I might be able to relax and enjoy myself a little bit more.'

"The medium-sized bull said, 'Funny you should mention that— I've been thinking the same thing. It seems like I just can't get anything done anymore because I'm always tied up with those cows of mine. If I could get rid of the responsibility for about 5 of my cows, I think I could be a lot more productive.'

"About that time the two older bulls noticed that the youngest bull was kicking up a heck of a fuss behind them. He was snorting and throwing his head back and forth and kicking grass up as high as he could into the air behind him.

"The oldest bull said, 'What in the world do you think you're doing — can't you see the size of that home boy?'

"The youngest bull stopped kicking long enough to look at the oldest bull and say, 'Hell yes I can see him — I just want him to know that I'm a *BULL!*'"

The hotel van showed up about that time and the driver gave Susan the strangest look when he heard her tell Rob, "What a bunch of bull!"

Cars, Bars & War Stories

I got to fly a European training mission with my reserve squadron last year. A half dozen pilot friends of mine (representing nearly all of the major US airlines) and a dozen or so flight engineers and load masters, took a C-5 to Europe for a week of exceptionally valuable training sorties.

We got a great deal accomplished, and had a ball doing it. Naturally, over the course of a week's flying together, we managed to swap a couple of pretty good stories.

The colonels on the crew, Ron and Robbie, supplied the political humor during the trip (Ron is a card-carrying Republican, and Robbie is a Democrat). Robbie started it — we were in base operations at Frankfurt when Robbie said, "Say Ron, do you know the difference between Dan Quayle and Jane Fonda?"

Ron looked at Robbie sideways, (sort of like the way a dog looks at you when you make a noise he doesn't understand), then Ron said, "No, what's the difference?"

Robbie said, "Jane Fonda *did* go to Vietnam."

At the time of our trip, the list of Democratic presidential contenders had been whittled down to one, Michael Dukakis, but the names of the other recent contenders were still fresh in the public's mind. Gary Hart's adventure aboard the Monkey Business was still fairly recent news, and Joe Biden's experiment with plagiarism was still a source of embarrassment for many Democrats.

At any rate, that was the avenue of retaliation that Ron chose when he asked Robbie, "Did you hear that story about Richard Nixon, Jimmy Carter, Gary Hart, and Joe Biden on the cruise ship?"

It was Robbie's turn to glance askance at Ron, but Ron went right ahead with his story. Ron said, "It seems that all four men were sharing a drink in the ship's bar, when the ship suddenly struck an iceberg and began to sink.

"As soon as they realized that the life boats were being lowered into the water, Jimmy took charge of the situation and commanded, 'Everyone into the boats — women and children first.'

"Tricky Dick responded with, 'Screw the women and children.'

"To which Gary Hart immediately replied, 'Do you think we have time?'

"Joe Biden put down his drink and said, 'Do you think we have time?'"

Robbie got in the last shot before we left base ops — he tapped

Ron on the elbow and said, "Did you see that movie about Dan Quayle's Vietnam war experiences? They called it: *Full Dinner Jacket.*"

Ron was just opening his mouth to retaliate, but Robbie kept him off balance by asking, "You heard what Dan said when they asked him what he thought about the Roe vs. Wade case, didn't you?"

Before Ron could regroup, Robbie said, "Dan looked at the reporters and said, 'Oh yes, Roe versus Wade — best presidential decision ever made. It dealt with Washington's decision to cross the Delaware, didn't it?'"

Those two kept at each other for the entire week, but I think Ron finally told the best story of the trip. I was somewhat of an unwitting accomplice on his last story — I told a car story that reminded Ron of his tale. It all occurred in the Indian restaurant in Mildenhall Village, England, where all of the pilots congregated on the last night of the trip for a curry dinner.

The food was great, and the conversation finally turned to the type of British sports car which nearly ran down Dennis Minder and I in the street outside the restaurant before dinner. (We were playing team tin-can soccer in the street while we waited for the restaurant to open, and the score was tied — we forgot that they drive on the wrong side of the road over there.)

All the talk about cars reminded me of my classmate in 737 school, Phil Amrhein, and his story about starting his car in the middle of a Pittsburgh winter.

Phil and I were having a brew one night in Sewickley, Pennsylvania, when Phil told me that he lived in Sewickley during his probationary year at US Air. Of course he wasn't making any money to speak of during that probationary year, so his wife (of 2 months) was working in Pittsburgh to supplement their income.

They were making out all right — they rented a nice apartment on top of a huge, scenic hill, and Phil had some money saved up to help get them through the year. The one point where they were hurting, was in the transportation category.

Phil's used car was not in terrific mechanical condition and, since they could only afford to keep one car, they were constantly juggling their schedules so that they could get to work. The car's battery was old and nearly worn out, but they couldn't afford to replace it. Phil knew just how to work the accelerator to get the car started before the battery ran out of juice, even on the coldest mornings.

Phil returned from an all-night red-eye one frigid January morning and just barely managed to get the car started in the employee parking lot before the battery ran down. He drove it home over the icy roads and parked it in the driveway directly below the bedroom window of their apartment. His wife was just shutting off the alarm clock when Phil stumbled into the bedroom and fell into the bed.

His wife often had trouble starting the car on cold mornings, so Phil forced himself to remain half conscious while she prepared to go to work. She kissed him good-bye, then he heard their apartment door close, followed shortly by the sound of the car door slamming shut.

A low moan escaped from his throat as Phil listened to the car's starter, "Haruh, haruh, haruh — haaruuh, haruuh, haaruhh — haaaruuuh, haaaruuuh, haaruuuh — haaaaruuuuh..."

The sound of the car door closing was much louder this time than it had been a couple of minutes earlier. Phil could hear his wife's curses long before the apartment door opened — they only grew louder as she marched into their bedroom.

"It's Ok, it's Ok," he told her, "I'll get up and get it started — don't worry, I can start it."

Of course he still had to listen to her harangues while he got dressed and found his keys, but within 5 minutes he was ready to go downstairs and start the car for her. Unfortunately, the battery was too depleted even for Phil's expert technique.

For a minute or so, Phil listened to his wife rant about being fired, then he said, "Ok, we can still push-start it — you *do* know how to start a rolling car, don't you?"

If Phil expected anything but a sharp retort from his wife deriding his insinuations of incompetence — then he should have phrased the question a little differently. Without further explanations, Phil held the door open while his wife took her place behind the wheel, then he sloshed through the snow to the front of the car so he could push it back into the street.

He only lost his footing twice while pushing the car backwards, which he figured was pretty good on the unshoveled driveway. When the car was pointed down the huge hill, Phil took up his station behind the car and shouted, "Are you ready?"

His wife immediately shouted back, "I've been ready for the past half hour, it's this darn car that's not ready!"

Phil bit his lip, he knew they would only have one chance at starting the car — if it didn't work, the car would be stranded at the bottom of the hill, about 5 miles from their apartment.

When he was certain his voice would sound calm, Phil shouted, "You have the transmission in second gear, don't you honey?"

He heard the clutch linkages work and the transmission clunk, then his wife's voice again, "Of course I have the darn transmission in second gear."

Phil said, "Ok, the key is on, isn't it?"

His wife answered, "**YES,** the damn key is on — how could I have steered out of the driveway without the key on?"

Phil leaned his shoulder against the trunk, but the car didn't move, so he shouted, "You will have to press in the clutch so I can start it rolling."

He heard the clutch linkages depress again, then his wife answered, "I know that!"

Phil leaned against the car again, and this time it started to roll. The hill was fairly level on the very top (where he was starting from), so it took nearly all of his strength to push the car to the beginning of the hill's steep slope.

Twice his feet slipped out from under him as he pushed against the icy street, and he found himself face down in the snow. He cracked his elbow against the rear bumper when he fell the second time, but he got up and finally had the car rolling down the steep part of the hill.

It didn't take long before the car was rolling faster than Phil could run, and once again he found his weight too far forward of his feet to remain upright. This time he picked himself up from the street and shouted after the rapidly accelerating car, "Try it! Try it! Try it!"

At first he was afraid that he was too far away for his wife to hear him, but then she responded. To Phil's dismay, he heard the engine's starter, "Haaaruuuh, haaaruuuh, haaruuuh — haaaaruuuuh..."

The car was far too distant by that time for his wife to hear his pleas to, "Let out the clutch!," so he just stood there with his hands on his hips and watched the car race to the bottom of the hill. If it hadn't been for the significant cooling-off period that the hike back up the hill provided, Phil's marriage might never have seen it's first anniversary.

Listening to Phil's story reminded Ron of an incident that happened to one of his neighbors in Austin, an insurance salesman named Bob Whitley.

It seemed that Bob made a sales call on a family who lived in an apartment complex which had very limited parking facilities. Bob was forced to park on the side of the road across from the apartments. That was where all visitors parked. As a matter of fact, Bob parked directly behind the heavily-chromed, customized, 3/4-ton pickup truck of another visitor.

The brake pedal on Bob's car had a bad habit of sticking in the down position, which would cause the brake lights to remain illuminated and run down the battery while Bob was making his sales calls. That is exactly the condition that Bob found when he finished his business in the apartment complex and returned to his car.

Bob was just about to go back to his client's apartment and call for a wrecker, when he noticed a scantily-clad young blonde crossing the road with a set of keys in her hand. She inserted a key into the driver's door of the pickup in front of him, then high-stepped up into the truck's raised cab.

Bob immediately climbed out of his car and walked up to her window. When she saw Bob approaching the truck, the blonde rolled down the window, put on a big Texas smile, and said, "Hi."

Bob said, "Hi. My battery is dead, would you mind giving me a jump start?"

She said, "No, I don't mind at all, as long as you know how to hook up the battery cables — I'm afraid that I don't know anything about that kind of stuff."

Bob said, "No problem, I know exactly how to do it. Are the cables behind your seat?"

The blue-eyed beauty said, "No, this is my boyfriend's truck and I know that he doesn't keep any jumper cables in here — don't you have a set in your car?"

Bob said, "No, I don't. I thought you might have some in the truck."

She said, "No, I'm sorry."

Bob glanced around while he tried to come up with another idea for starting his car, and he noticed that the truck had an enormous, custom, wooden front bumper on it.

Bob said, "Say, do you suppose your boyfriend would mind if you gave me a push start?"

The blonde said, "I'm sure he wouldn't mind, but I don't know how to do that."

Bob said, "There's nothing to it, you just get behind my car and push me fast enough so that my engine will turn over. Your front bumper is so big that I'm sure it will match up with my rear bumper just fine. The only thing that might be just a little bit tricky, is the fact that my car has an automatic transmission. We might have to get it up to 40 or 45 miles-per-hour before the torque converter starts spinning fast enough to turn over my engine — do you feel comfortable with doing that?"

She smiled and said, "Sure, I drive faster than that all the time."

Bob said, "Thanks, I sure do appreciate it," then he went back to

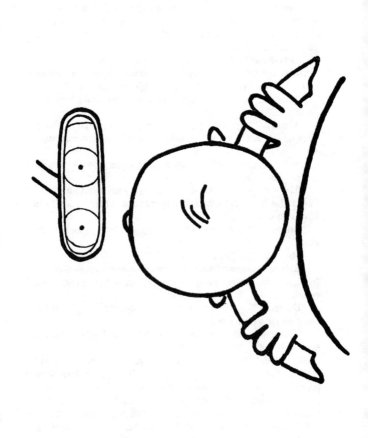

his car to get ready.

The blonde started the big pickup and swung it around in the road to get behind Bob while he slid back into place in the driver's seat of his car. Bob thought, "I'd better make sure that everything is ready before she starts pushing me," so he began preflighting his car to make sure it was set up properly.

First, he made sure that the emergency brake handle between the seats was in the full down position. Then, Bob placed the shift lever into the DRIVE position, and made certain the key was on, so he would be able to steer.

Bob thought, "I'd better roll down my window so I can stick my arm out and wave to let her know when the engine starts," so he grasped the window handle and began turning it counter-clockwise. While he was rolling down the window, Bob glanced in the rear view mirror to see how the blonde was doing... he was aghast to see the huge wooden bumper racing toward him at the head of a huge cloud of billowing dust!

Inside the pickup, the blonde's eyes were fixed on the speedometer, ensuring that the needle was exactly over the numerals "45" at the moment of impact.

Bob leaned on the horn, but witnesses said his yells were drowning out the horn when they hit... *"WHAM!"*

Needless to say, Bob's car never started again.

Cutter & Shooter's Airline Interview

Warnie Meisetschleager is one of those airline pilots of the 1980s who got kicked in the teeth several times, and somehow managed to keep on smiling. When I first met Warnie (we call him M+14 around my reserve squadron because nobody can pronounce Meisetschleager) he was a very popular Captain at Transtar. Now, he's a flight engineer for Delta. The thing that keeps guys like Warnie going is their sense of humor.

I flew a local with Warnie a couple of weeks ago, (Okay, for everyone who didn't read the first book — a "local" is Air Force Reserve slang for a training mission flown in the local flying area) and Warnie started entertaining us with his ideas as to what this year's "Cutter & Shooter" story should be about *("Cutter & Shooter"* and *"Larry's Airline Interview"* were Warnie's favorite stories in: *The Aviation Humor of 1987).*

Anyway, Warnie managed to fly a flawless engine-out, back-course localizer, cross-panel approach in a C-5 while he told us this story, and the engineers laughed so hard that I couldn't resist making it this year's entry in the "Cutter & Shooter" category.

So, here's Warnie's version of: *Cutter & Shooter's Airline Interview.*

In Warnie's modern-day version of the Cutter & Shooter saga, we find Cutter and Shooter making a living as reserve bums in an obscure C-5 squadron in southern Texas.

They're getting a little tired of putting up with some of the harassment that reserve bums have to live with, so Cutter finally convinces Shooter that it's time for them to put in an airline application. Of course Shooter is hesitant to do anything that might break up the team, but he finally agrees to Cutter's plan, after Cutter tells him to they will file a "joint application". Their application will carry the stipulation that any airline that hires one of them — must hire both of them.

Cutter does a little research, and quickly learns that Northwest Airlines is the highest paying pilot employer, so Cutter rifles off an application to Northwest.

About a week later, an invitation to report to Minneapolis for an interview with Northwest shows up in Cutter and Shooters' mailbox. Of course both of the famous pilots are delighted at the news, especially since Northwest had apparently agreed to their stipulation that they come as a set, or not at all.

The daring duo appeared in Minnesota on the appointed day, and quickly found themselves absorbed in a regimen of physical, written, and simulator evaluations. They helped each other out where ever they could, and all apparently went well throughout the day. Their last hurdle was the dreaded interview with the head of the personnel department, Mr. Vargo.

Late afternoon found Cutter, Shooter, and a half dozen other pilot candidates, nervously killing time in the waiting room outside Mr. Vargo's office. When Mr. Vargo finally arrived for the interviews, both Cutter and Shooter noticed that there was something strange about his appearance.

When Mr. Vargo walked through the waiting area to enter his office, Cutter noticed that his hair seemed to be abnormally long on the sides. Shooter unconsciously stroked the side of his own head, when he noticed that Mr. Vargo's hair didn't lay against the sides of his scalp just right.

Cutter was just about to ask Shooter if he noticed anything funny about Mr. Vargo's hair, when Vargo opened his office door and called out, "Mr. Rubeor?"

A tall, handsome applicant sitting in the corner of the room immediately said, "Here sir."

Mr. Vargo said, "Would you step into my office please?"

Rubeor smiled and said, "Certainly," then he picked up his briefcase and followed Vargo into his office.

Inside, Mr. Vargo motioned toward a chair in front of his desk and said, "Make yourself comfortable Mr. Rubeor — this is just a little formality that we go through to make sure that we have all of the information we need to evaluate your application fairly."

Rubeor said, "I understand," but while he was speaking, he couldn't take his eyes off of Vargo's head. Now that he was looking at Vargo's face straight-on, he could see that the reason his hair looked strange, was because Vargo did not have any external ears!

Mr. Vargo said, "I always like to start off my pilot candidate interviews with a little observation test. I find it's a great ice-breaker. For instance, have you noticed anything unusual about my appearance?"

Rubeor's mind shifted into warp-drive. *"What is he looking for,"* he wondered, *"does he really want to know if I'm observant enough to notice that he doesn't have any ears? Is it a test to see if I'm sharp enough to notice other air-traffic that ATC hasn't called to us? Or, is this a test to see if I'm too timid to say anything — the kind of copilot who would let his Captain land gear-up? Or, maybe he wants to know if I'm a tactful person. Maybe it's a test to see if I'm considerate enough of other people's misfortunes — if I'll have problems getting along with my coworkers."*

Finally, Rubeor decided to give up on trying to out-guess Vargo, so he defaulted to his standard philosophy: "Honesty is the best policy."

Rubeor said, "Well Mr. Vargo, I'm not really sure about what you're asking me. If you honestly want to know whether I'm observant enough to notice that you don't have any ears — then, I can tell you that I did notice that fact. I wasn't going to say anything about it though."

Rubeor was stunned at Vargo's violent reaction. Vargo instantly ripped Rubeor's employment folder in half, then threw it at him!

Vargo's face was flushed with anger as he said, "Get *out* of my office! You're never going to work for this airline, you insensitive, ignorant, barbarian!"

Rubeor said, "Please Mr. Vargo — I certainly didn't mean to offend you..."

Vargo pointed toward a side door and cut Rubeor off in mid-sentence with, "I said get out of my office! Leave by that side door — I don't want the other candidates to become *contaminated* by *you!"*

Rubeor stood and said, "I'm sorry if I offended you, I certainly did not intend to — good-day sir," then Rubeor made a dignified exit out the side door.

After taking a few moments to compose himself, Mr. Vargo opened the door to the waiting area and said, "Is there a Mr. Cutter here?"

Cutter immediately said, "Right here sir."

Vargo smiled and said, "Would you step into my office please?"

Cutter followed Vargo into the office and made himself comfortable in the same chair Rubeor had sat in. Vargo seemed exceptionally friendly as he explained the purpose of the interview, but Cutter couldn't help but wonder why he hadn't seen Rubeor exit the office.

Finally, Vargo said, "I always like to start off my pilot candidate interviews with a little observation test. I find it's a great ice breaker. For instance, have you noticed anything unusual about my appearance?"

Cutter's mind immediately began racing at full speed — he went through exactly the same mental processes that Rubeor had, and finally came to the same conclusion.

Cutter said, "Well Mr. Vargo, I did notice that you must have been in an accident of some sort, or perhaps suffered a birth defect."

Vargo looked at Cutter quizzically.

Cutter said, "What I'm trying to say is, that I did notice that you don't appear to have any external ears."

Vargo's reaction was even more violent than the last time! He jumped up out of his chair and threw Cutter's application folder at him, then yelled, "You rude, uncivilized, atrocious savage! I've never encountered such an uncouth group of inhuman brutes! You can rest assured that no one as cruel as yourself will *ever* work for this airline — get *out* of my office!"

Cutter raised his hands and said, "Now hold on a minute Mr. Vargo, I sure didn't mean to..."

Vargo pointed at the side door and interrupted Cutter with, "I said... get the hell out of my office!"

Cutter could see his apology was wasted, so he quickly exited via the office's side door. After he was outside the office, a thought occurred to Cutter, "Say, wait a minute. *If I can still get old Shooter hired, they'll have to hire me too! I'll bet Vargo doesn't know about that stipulation in our application.*"

One problem remained however — Cutter was certain that Shooter would answer Vargo's observation question the same way he had. There was only one thing to do — Cutter had to find his way back to the waiting area and warn Shooter.

Cutter's intrinsic sense of direction helped him find his way through the maze of hallways, until he was finally standing just outside the doorway to the waiting area. Cutter could see Shooter inside, sitting at the end of the couch.

Cutter didn't want to expose himself inside the waiting area, just in case Mr. Vargo opened the door to his office. So, Cutter stood in the hallway, just outside the waiting area, and whispered, "Pssst — Shooter!"

At first Shooter didn't respond, so Cutter whispered again, slightly louder this time, "Pssst — Shooter!"

This time Shooter heard him and looked up from his magazine. When Shooter saw Cutter standing in the hallway, a concerned frown creased his forehead.

Cutter pointed to his ears and whispered, "Don't say anything about his ears!"

Shooter didn't completely understand, he shook his head and whispered, "What?"

Cutter pointed to his ears again and said, "Don't say anything about his ears — he's really sensitive about his ears!"

Shooter heard him this time — he nodded his head and whispered, "Got it."

Just then, the office door opened and Mr. Vargo stepped out. Cutter was grateful that he had remained out of sight, as he listened to Vargo say, "Do we have a Mr. Shooter here?"

Shooter gave Cutter a quick wink, then turned to face Mr. Vargo and said, "Right here sir."

Vargo said, "Hi, would you step into my office please?"

Shooter said, "Certainly," and followed Vargo inside. Vargo explained the purpose of the interview while Shooter crossed his legs and settled into the interviewee's chair.

Shooter was composed and prepared when Vargo finally said, "I always like to start off my pilot candidate interviews with a little observation test. I find it's a great ice-breaker. For instance, have you noticed anything at all unusual about my appearance?"

Shooter sat with a thoughtful expression on his face for a few moments, then he said, "Well sir, I did notice... that you're wearing contact lenses."

A smile of astonishment and joy instantly spread across Vargo's face. Vargo chuckled lightly, then said, "That is an outstanding observation! Very few people notice that I'm wearing contact lenses — I think part of the reason is because I wear clear contacts. This is my true eye color — I don't try to change it with cosmetically colored contacts."

Shooter smiled politely, and Vargo reiterated, "That really is an excellent observation on your part."

Shooter said, "Oh, it's really more of a deduction than an observation."

Vargo said, "Oh?"

Shooter said, "Yea — I figured; shoot... you don't have anyplace to *hang* a pair of glasses!"

You may not find it too surprising to learn — that Cutter and Shooter are both still bumming it in the reserves in a C-5 Reserve squadron in Southern Texas.

Drugs, Turkeys, and Rock & Roll

If Francis Lorennzo ever leaves the airline business, I'm certain he will enter the commercial helicopter business. Some of the cheapest, most labor-abusive managements in the United States are found in the commercial helicopter industry.

Most of the commercial helicopter operators pay their pilots woefully inadequate wages, and few provide any kind of retirement benefits. I know what you're thinking — that the true definition of an optimist should be "a single-engine helicopter pilot who is worried about a retirement plan" — but there is no excuse for the low pay and benefits that these pilots receive, especially when their qualifications are so high.

I think all of us would want the most highly-qualified med-evac pilots available if we were asking them to evacuate *our* families from a night-time accident in the mountains.

Anyway — for years I've been hearing stories from my friends in the industry about the abusive treatment these helicopter operators dish out, so it does my heart good to hear about one of the pilots getting "one-up" on them. My old stick buddy Dave Denham just told me such a story — so I thought I would share it with you.

Before going to work as an Emergency Medical Service (EMS) helicopter pilot in Denver, Dave used to work in the Gulf of Mexico for a company called Opti Flight. Opti was owned and operated by a gentleman who was rumored to have been Frank Lorenzo's brother-in-law, a Mr. Jeremy Davidson.

Davidson paid his helicopter pilots wages which were far lower than the local taxi drivers earned — but he did promise full medical benefits to any pilot that would work for him.

The fact that the medical benefits began only 30 days after signing on with the company, was the primary reason that LJ Weslow went to work for Opti. LJ's wife, Debbie, was pregnant when he got out of the Army, and he wanted to make certain he had full medical coverage for her delivery.

Exactly 34 days after LJ signed on with Opti, Debbie gave birth to a bouncing baby boy. The medical tab for the delivery came to $3,500. LJ paid the medical bill, then submitted a reimbursement claim to Opti — just as Davidson had instructed him to do.

A couple of weeks after LJ submitted the claim, he was called upon to fly a team of medical people out to one of the many large oil-drilling rigs in the Gulf of Mexico. LJ did not know or care, that the medical team he was flying to the oil rig was actually a drug-testing team.

The oil company which operated the oil rig had contracted with an independent medical company to test the workers on the oil rig for drugs — LJ's job was simply to fly them to the rig and back.

After LJ landed on the oil rig, he proceeded to make himself comfortable in the recreation area of the oil rig while the drug testing team went about their work.

LJ is a big rock & roll fan, one of those guys who really gets into his music. As far as LJ was concerned, everything was "ops normal" — but when the drug team noticed him dancing around the pool table, beating out the rhythm of the Rolling Stones' *Honky Tonk Women* on his cue stick... they decided he was an excellent candidate for their "wee wee in the bottle" test.

Of course, LJ wasn't too fond of that idea — not that he had anything to hide, but like any red-blooded, aggressive, independent, self-confident American helicopter pilot — he didn't like being told that he had to urinate in their darn bottle!

So, LJ informed the drug team that he was not an employee of the oil company that they were under contract to test — that he worked for Opti Flight, which was an independent contractor to the oil company, just like they were.

The drug team leader told LJ that they were instructed to test everyone on the rig. LJ told him that Opti Flight had its own drug-testing policy, and he was under no obligation to submit to the oil company's policies.

Well, egos and tempers started playing a bigger role in the argument than common sense did, and pretty soon the drug team leader told LJ that if he did not submit to the test, that he would be treated as if he had tested positive for drugs, which meant that he could no longer function as an employee of the company. That meant that a new pilot would have to be flown out to recover the drug testing team and LJ's helicopter.

LJ had his dander up by now, so there was no way he was going to pee in a bottle for those guys.

A cooler head somewhere in the group finally suggested that they call LJ's boss, and they did. The first person they got in touch with at Opti Flight was the chief pilot, Rob. After listening to the drug team leader's threats, Rob told LJ to take the test.

LJ refused, so Rob got in touch with Davidson and explained the situation to him. Instead of standing up for his employee, Davidson called LJ and told him to take the test.

LJ probably was a bit bull-headed about the situation, but he already had his mind made up that he wasn't going to take that test. What were they going to do, fire him from that lousy job?

LJ told Davidson to have some balls and tell the druggies to drop dead, but instead Davidson dispatched a relief pilot to recover the team and LJ's helicopter. Davidson told LJ to turn in his wings and his shoulder boards as soon as he landed.

Well, in the process of rounding up a relief pilot to go get LJ, the entire story quickly spread through the pilot ranks. As soon as they learned that LJ had been fired, they all decided to quit. That's a fairly common trait in companies that abuse their employees — most of them are usually looking for an excuse to quit.

When Davidson saw his entire pilot force walk into his office behind LJ with their wings and shoulder boards in their hands, he quickly reversed his decision to terminate LJ — he knew there were better ways to hurt him.

LJ quickly tired of the shoddy treatment he received from Rob and Davidson, but he soon discovered that he couldn't leave. Davidson stopped payment on LJ's $3,500 medical claim, and LJ didn't have enough in savings to support Debbie and his son until he could find a new job.

LJ became your basic disgruntled, antagonistic employee — his favorite come-back to Rob's snide comments about broke pilots, was to chastise him and the company for being too cheap to buy the employees a Christmas ham or turkey.

With Christmas approaching rapidly, it greatly irritated all of the pilots to know that the company was too cheap to even buy them a Christmas turkey.

LJ became so vocal about the issue, that Rob finally decided to do something about it — he resolved to come up with some practical joke that would turn the tables on LJ whenever he mouthed-off about not getting a Christmas turkey.

Debbie just happened to be in the office, picking up LJ's pay check, the day that Rob was brainstorming his practical joke. Rob didn't know who Debbie was, so he was unconcerned about the fact that she overheard him telling his secretary his plans for the practical joke.

Rob told his secretary to go buy a huge gift-wrapped box, and the smallest Cornish game hen she could find — they would put the hen inside the box and present it to LJ the following day as his "Christmas Turkey."

When Debbie got home, she found LJ playing cards with one of her girlfriends, Tess, while he babysat their son.

Tess liked to spend her evenings hanging out with the single helicopter pilots of the company in the local bars, but she spent most of her days with Debbie and LJ and their son, whom she adored.

When Debbie told LJ and Tess what she had overheard at the office, she expected LJ to be mad — but he wasn't. Nothing could spoil the excitement he felt. Just before Debbie got home, LJ had received a phone call. The call relayed the news that he had just been hired by a new EMS company which treated its people much better than Opti treated theirs.

Tess was the one who really got her dander up when she heard about Rob's snide trick, and she was the one who thought up the comeback. Tess excused herself, saying that she had to go to the fabric store and purchase some black and white cloth, so she could do a little sewing that night.

The following day, Tess was waiting with LJ and Debbie in their home when Rob called to tell LJ that he could come by the office and pick up his Christmas turkey. LJ told him he would be right in to get it.

When they arrived at the office, Tess waited in the car for 10 minutes while LJ went in to get his turkey.

Rob made LJ wait a few minutes, so he could assemble the entire office staff for the big moment. When everyone was present, Rob pulled the huge brightly-wrapped box from under the counter and said, "Here you go LJ, here's the Christmas turkey you deserve for all your wonderful work around here."

LJ glanced at his watch to make sure the timing would work right, then he said, "Well, thank you Rob. You don't know how much I appreciate this... it really makes me feel good to know that this is the kind of company that cares about its employees ... the type of place that you're proud to work for."

Rob grinned and winked at his secretary, then said, "Open it up LJ, I'm sure everyone would like to see your turkey."

LJ knew that Tess would be walking through the door any second, so he started unwrapping the box as he said, "Rob, I want you to know that many, many people will appreciate this generous gift."

Rob said, "What?"

LJ said, "Well you see, Debbie and I really didn't want this turkey for ourselves," LJ could see Tess closing the door behind her now, being careful not to shut it on her long black dress, "we really just wanted to be able to give something to the poor orphans down at Sister Teresa's orphanage."

LJ finished tearing open the top of the box — the look of stunned surprise on his face should have won him an Oscar as he held the tiny Cornish game hen up where everyone could see it.

Tess made her way though the office crowd until she was standing in front of LJ.

LJ looked at Tess in her full nun outfit, then back down at the pitiful game bird in his hand and stammered, "I'm, I'm ... I'm sorry Sister Teresa — when I told you I was donating a turkey for your Christmas dinner, I thought it would be a real turkey."

Tess took the bird from LJ's trembling hands and said, "That's all right Mister Weslow — the children will be eternally grateful for anything that they receive."

LJ said, "I'm sorry Sister — I'll drive you home now."

Just before closing the door, LJ turned back to face Rob and said, "Tell Davidson that I quit, and the last thing I'm going to do in this town is call Channel 4 and get their news team out to the orphanage this afternoon to cover this terrific donation from Opti Flight."

Tess and LJ left the office in a stunned silence — Rob's chin was practically touching his chest. As soon as Tess and LJ were gone, the office workers exploded in a flurry of anger against Rob and his cruel joke.

The bedlam in the outer office soon grew loud enough to disturb Davidson, who stormed out of his office demanding to know what all the noise was about. When the secretaries told him what had happened, Davidson immediately fired Rob — then ordered a dozen of the largest turkeys in the grocery store delivered to the real Sister Teresa's orphanage.

LJ left town the day after Christmas for his new job — it took his attorney almost a year to get the $3,500 from Davidson, but he did receive interest and attorney's fees in addition to the $3,500.

Davidson got to make an unscheduled TV appearance in front of a baffled Channel 4 news team, and the even more confused (but grateful) real Sister Teresa.

All of the pilots who worked at Opti at that time have since moved on to better jobs, and Tess — well, she developed an entirely new habit.

"G' Day, Let's Mate"

I have a hard time understanding Australians. I don't mean their dress or behavior, that's obvious enough. I mean that sometimes, I literally have a difficult time interpreting their speech.

I didn't really mind it too much the first time that I encountered the problem. As a matter of fact, it helped me sell several books. I was working my booth at the Oshkosh airshow in '88, when a lovely young lady in khaki shorts strolled by.

It was a little slow at the moment, so I decided to see if she could drum up a little business for our booth. (Little did I know just how successful I would be.)

She smiled when she read the title of my book, *"The Aviation Humor of 1987"*. A quizzical expression spread over her face as she shifted her purse higher onto her shoulder so she could use both hands to examine one of the books.

I watched silently while she quickly flipped through the pages. (One thing I learned early, was that you can kill as many book sales as you save by spouting off too early.) As soon as she realized that there weren't any pictures in the book, she placed it back onto the table and started to step away.

Now was the time to save the sale.

"Have you read anything about this book lately?" I asked.

She smiled charmingly as she looked back at me, and replied with an unmistakable Australian accent, "No, I aven't."

I quickly snatched up the copy of the latest *Flying* magazine and held it out so she could read the classified advertisement it contained for *The Aviation Humor of 1987*.

When she finished perusing the ad, I said, "As you can see, we have to charge our mail-order customers a postage and handling fee — which you can save by purchasing the book directly from us here at the booth today. Also, if you buy today, you can get a personal inscription written in the front of the book by the author, at no extra charge."

Her beautiful brown eyes opened wide as she said, "Are you the author?"

I picked up a copy of the book and held it with the back cover turned toward her, so she could see that it was my picture on the back of the book.

After reading her smile of recognition, I flipped the book open. It happened to open to page 42, which was the beginning of a short story called, *A Tough May Day.*

I handed the book to her and said, "I'll make you a wager—if you can read this story without laughing out loud, I'll give you the book."

She immediately started chuckling, then somewhat-reluctantly took the book from my hands. The people closest to the booth heard her little chuckle as well as my offer, so a few of them turned toward the booth and began picking up copies of the book to peruse for themselves.

The young lady was just finishing the first page when I said, "See, this is already good for business. Anytime people see a beautiful young woman laughing out loud as she reads a book—they can't help but become interested in the book themselves."

She laughed again to relieve her nervousness, and more people started picking up copies of the book. She had a wonderful sense of humor. About halfway down the second page she encountered a line which tickled her. As if on cue, she laughed with one of those lovely, contagious laughs that some lucky people possess. Several onlookers couldn't help but chuckle themselves, although they had no idea what she was laughing about.

I said, "I don't think I'm going to have to give you this book,"

She laughed again. More people picked up copies of the book, and a few of the earlier takers began chuckles of their own.

My lady friend was growing embarrassed about being the center of attention, so she closed the book and said, "Oh all right, I'll take it. But, can you sign it to my boyfriend?"

I said, "Sure, I'll sign it to all of your boyfriends if you like."

She smiled as she handed me the book and said, "Just one will do, thank you."

I opened the book to the inside front cover and said, "Okay, what is the lucky guy's name?"

It was at this point, that I started losing control of the situation. The lady said, "His name is Chuck Somato."

I like to keep people talking while I sign their books. So, as I began writing I said, "That's an unusual name, is he Japanese?"

I discovered later that her one-word reply was, "Czechoslovakian." But, that's not what I heard at the time. I heard, "Chuck Sovaken."

Thinking I must have misunderstood her the first time, I stopped writing, looked up at her, then asked, "Chuck Sovaken?"

She seemed a little surprised by my inquisitive tone of voice, but she quickly insisted, "Yes—Czechoslovakian."

Well, I still wasn't hearing her clearly, but several folks in the audience did understand her by then. (When I thought about it later, I realized that this situation is one of the all-time favorites of comedy writers. The audience understands what both of the actors are saying, but the actors just can't get there. Remember, "Who's on first?")

Her tone of voice was very emphatic, so I bent down to write again and said, "Okay, I'll sign this to Chuck Sovaken."

She immediately said, "No, don't do that! Sign it to Chuck Somato!"

I glanced up and said, "The Japanese guy?"

Once again I heard her bewildered voice insist, "No — **He's Chuck Sovaken!**"

The crowd was loving it. I said, "So you want two books? One for Chuck Sovaken, and one for the Japanese guy?"

The crowd couldn't take it anymore. The young lady seemed mildly amused by their guffaws and knee slaps, but she couldn't quite unlock her lower jaw long enough to join in the laughter. I was completely baffled.

Finally, a fellow in the front of the crowd gained control of himself and said, "Her boyfriend's name is Chuck Somato — and he is from Czech-o-slo-vak-i-a!"

The wide-eyed expression of cognizance that lit up my face only added to the hilarity of the crowd. Fortunately, my lady friend also realized what had happened, and she joined in the laughter.

I sold more books in the next 30 minutes than I had in the prior two days!

I had a similar experience in Texas in mid-August of 1989. My wife and daughter were visiting family in Missouri. I was spending the night with our friends Ed and Jane Dingivan, in San Antonio. It was almost midnight when their neighbor, Bill, dropped in for a nightcap.

Bill had just returned from a visit with his parents in his native Australia, and he was suffering a nearly-terminal case of jet lag. I'm afraid that during his trip, Bill's Aussie-Tex accent took a distinct turn toward the "roo" section of his vocabulary.

The most troublesome characteristic of the Australian accent for me, is their tendency to chop off the first syllable or two of words which they find unnecessarily long and difficult (such as "good" and "have").

Ed and Jane and I were listening to Bill describe his recent trip home, when he suddenly changed the subject. (The last time I had seen Bill was just prior to our move to North Carolina.) Bill turned to me and asked, "All settled in N.C. yet?"

I said, "All the boxes aren't unpacked yet, but I suppose we're reasonably settled in."

Bill said, "Wha's the weather like — 'ot and 'umid I imagine?"

I said, "Actually it's been very pleasant the past couple of weeks. We have a nice deck on the back of our house, and we've been spending a lot of time out there in the evenings — barbecuing, reading, and just hanging out."

Bill's next question threw me off, not only because of the way that he pronounced the words, but also because of the way that he worded the question. You see, if an American wanted to know if the bugs were a problem while you hung out on your deck, he would say something like, "Are the mosquitoes very bad over there?" or "Don't the bugs eat you alive?" or something along those lines.

A true Australian would never suffer such verbosity. Bill managed to cut the same question down to two syllables.

Now, what Bill was trying to ask was, "Any insects?"

But, the three Americans in the room all heard the same question — *"Any sex?"*

I quickly resolved not to allow Bill's forward nature to throw me off balance. After all, Australia isn't the only country in the world with nude beaches.

I cleared my throat and said, "Not normally on the deck Bill. You see, the neighbors behind us have a clear view of our deck."

My, what a perplexed expression crossed Bill's face.

I was so busy gloating over my calm response, that I failed to notice Bill's worried expression. He quickly became preoccupied with visions of our North Carolina neighbors streaming over to our deck armed with fly swatters, cans of bug repellent, and whatever else it took to by-gosh keep those insects off the Morgans' back porch!

It was just too much for Bill to accept. Nobody has neighbors that good — not even in the Carolinas.

With an unmistakable note of disbelief in his voice, Bill looked me in the eye and asked, "The *neighbors* prevent it?"

By this time, Jane (who spent a lot more time around Bill than I) had figured out what was going on. Unfortunately, she couldn't think of a tactful way to illuminate the situation for me before I responded.

Thinking Bill's obvious disbelief was motivated by an unwillingness to believe that *anyone* could be so inhibited, I decided to fortify my explanation. So, I winked at Bill and said, "Well, the truth is—that my wife has been out of town since Tuesday!"

The beer slipped out of Bill's hand and smashed to the floor. I can only imagine the visions Bill conjured in response to that revelation.

My first clue that something was wrong was the sound of Ed's hysterical laughter as he collapsed into a corner of the kitchen.

Jane finally composed herself enough to pull her hands away from her beet-red face and tell me, "He asked you if there are any **INSECTS** on your deck!"

Bill (still wearing his befuddled expression) said, "What did you think I asked?"

It was my turn to laugh.

FIFI

A good friend of mine, Bob Reimard and his wife Alice, own the Alamo Aviation Art Gallery in San Antonio. It's located right across the street from the Alamo, in the Heart of Texas building.

Besides stocking a great aviation art collection, good old Bob has sold a lot of books for me. So, when he suggested that we share a booth at the Confederate Air Force's (C.A.F.) air show in Harlingen, Texas last year, I took him up on the offer. (Bob knows what he's talking about when it comes to making money at air shows.)

Well, we had a great time and did a fair amount of business, and Bob even came up with a pretty good story during a slow period in the air show.

Bob's story centers around one of the Confederate Air Force's many claims to fame, their B-29, "Fifi."

Fifi happens to be the only flyable B-29 left in the world, and the C.A.F. members are, rightly, very proud her.

In his story, Bob's WWII hero has persuaded some friends to make the trek to Harlingen with him to attend the annual air show. We join his group as he is blatantly trying to impress his younger friends with "slightly embellished" stories of his war-time exploits...

Mabel

Young Mabel from far-off Mt. Shasta,
Was marking her chart in Nebraska.
Her route was to Wooster,
But somebody goosed her,
And Mabel wound up in Alaska.

Flight Attendants With Crossed Legs

I'll be honest with you — I've never been much on racial, ethnic, or sexist jokes (I said *sexist*, not sex — I've actually always been sort of fond of sex jokes). It's always been too easy to get a *cheap* laugh with jokes that contained a racial or ethnic slur. If anybody can do it, where's the challenge?

There are exceptions though. Every once in awhile I get to fly with someone who can use these jokes in a self-deprecating sort of way that actually makes them sound pretty funny. It's still pretty dangerous ground though — even as good as Mark Twain was, he got his tit in the wringer a few times while working in this area.

Anyway, my buddy Abe and a couple of our flight attendants gave me such a good demonstration of this principle the other day, that I thought I would take another stab at it. A lot of people liked the Father John Munley stories in my first book, and his humor was basically the same as Abe's. (If you missed the first book, Father John was very fond of making fun of the way he was brought up in the Roman Catholic church.)

The last trip I flew on the 737-200 was with Captain Abe Goldstein and two of our more fun-loving flight attendants, Lori and Diane. When we called for our clearance, we were told we would have a 30 minute gate hold. With that much time to kill, Abe asked Lori to bring up a couple of cups of coffee.

Lori seldom does anything without Diane if she can help it, so we were soon sipping hot coffee with Lori and Diane in the cockpit. Both of them sat down on the jumpseat, crossed their legs, and proceeded to catch us up on the latest flight attendant stories going around the company.

Abe got them started when he said, "Any new stories going around the crew room these days?"

Lori and Diane exchanged clueless looks for a moment, then Diane said, "Have you heard the one about the 3 girls interviewing for a flight attendant's position?"

Abe said, "No, how does it go?"

Diane said, "Well, it seems that these 3 girls are all applying for the same job — one is from Atlanta, one is from Dallas, and the third is from Boston. The interviewer says, 'I'm going to ask all of you a hypothetical question, and I want you to tell me what you would do in this situation.'

"The three girls nodded, and the interviewer continued, 'Suppose that you were visiting someone in prison, and suddenly you find yourself caught in a riot. All of the guards are killed, and you find yourself the hostage of 5,000 prisoners. What would you do?'

"The girl from Atlanta says, 'Well, to save my honor, I suppose I would just have to kill myself.'

"The interviewer writes something on his pad, then turns to the Dallas girl and says, 'And what would you do?'

"The Dallas girl says, 'Well, I think I would pick out the biggest meanest inmate I could find, and make him my boyfriend, so the other prisoners would leave me alone.'

"The interviewer nodded and made a notation on his pad, then he turned to the Boston girl and said, 'And what would you do?'

"The Boston girl shrugged and said, 'I don't really see a problem.'"

I took a sip of coffee, then Abe took a sip of coffee. We looked at each other, then we looked at Lori — she shrugged. We finally looked at Diane — we were hoping that there was more to the story than that, but if there was, she wasn't letting on.

Abe put his coffee cup in the holder and checked that the parking brake was still set. Satisfied with the parking brake, Abe retrieved his coffee cup and finally turned around to look at Diane and said, "So... which one did he hire?"

Diane shrugged and said, "The one with no tits."

Abe was able to keep a straight face — I wasn't.

Abe countered with, "Do you know what you get when you cross Arnold Schwarzenegger with a Rabbi?"

Diane said, "What?"

Abe said, "Conan, the distributor."

Lori said, "Did you hear the one about the flight attendant and her husband who went camping?"

Abe chuckled and shook his head, so Lori said, "Well, this junior flight attendant had been working real hard, and she finally got a weekend off. So, she and her husband decided to go backpacking way up in the mountains, to get away from everything.

"They have a great time until the last night of their camping expedition, when her husband has to go to the bathroom during the middle of the night. Unfortunately, the poor guy accidentally steps on an extremely poisonous snake, and gets bitten twice.

"He kills the snake, then they get out their first aid book and look up what they should do for that kind of snake bite. The book says that there is no antidote — nothing can be done. The bitten party is certain to die within 12 hours.

"They know that they are too far from civilization to try to get any expert help, so the flight attendant says, 'What do you want to do?

"Her husband says, 'There is only one thing I want to do — I would like to make love to you one more time before I die.

"She consents to his request, and they make made passionate love in the sleeping bag. When they finish, she says, 'What do you want to do now?'

"Her husband says, 'I can't think of anything I would rather do — than make love to you one more time.'

"She is deeply touched, and they repeat their virtuoso performance. When they finish, the sleeping bag is practically torn to shreds. The flight attendant says, 'That was magnificent — what would you like to do now?'

"Her husband says, 'Well, if you don't mind — I'd like to make love to you one more time.'

"She says, 'Oh *sure* ... you don't have to get up in the morning!'"

Abe pulled a tissue from the box beside his seat and began wiping the glass faces of his flight instruments while he said, "Did you hear the one about the captain with cancer?"

Lori shook her head, so Abe said, "This captain is sitting in the flight surgeon's office, waiting for the doc to finish going over his lab results, and the doctor looks up and says, 'I'm sorry Bob, but your cancer is terminal — you only have 6 months to live.'

"The captain says, 'Six months! Isn't there anything I can do?'

"The doctor says, 'Well, you *could* marry a Jewish girl and move to Toledo.'

"The captain says, 'That will cure me?'

"The doctor says, 'No — but it will make the 6 months seem like a lifetime.'"

It was Diane's turn — she said, "Did you hear the one about the flight attendant with AIDS?"

That thought is enough to scare anyone — Abe managed to keep his cool and shake his head, so Diane said, "The doctor calls this flight attendant's husband into his office and says, 'I'm afraid I have some bad news for you — your wife either has AIDS, or a rare form of an extremely critical heart disease.'

"'I am planning to run a battery of tests to determine which condition she actually has — but I wanted to warn you first of the possibilities, so you could abstain from having sex with her. It will take about 2 weeks to complete all the tests.'

"Of course her husband is beside himself with anxiety — he

looks at the doc and says, 'Two weeks! Isn't there a faster test we can perform?'

"The doctor strokes his chin for a minute, then says, '"Yea, come to think of it, there is. You *could* tell her to run around the block as fast as she can. If she makes it — *don't screw her!*"

Why that story reminded Abe of the one that he told next is a mystery to me, but Abe said, "That's like the one about the Rabbi sitting in a bar in an airport terminal, waiting for his flight, when a hooker walks in and sits down at a table across the room from him.

"The hooker realizes that the Rabbi is eyeing her, so she finally gets up and slides into the other chair at the Rabbi's table, and says, 'For a hundred and fifty dollars, I'll do anything you want.'

"The Rabbi's eyebrows raise, and he says, 'Anything?'

"The hooker winks at him and nods her head, so the Rabbi immediately pulls out his checkbook and writes out a check for $150.

"The hooker looks over the check after the Rabbi slides it across the table to her, then she slips it into her blouse and says, 'Tell me what you want me to do baby.'

"The Rabbi starts to open his mouth, but she interrupts him and says, 'Tell me what you want... but just use three little words.'

"The Rabbi thinks about it a minute, then he leans close to her and whispers, *'Paint my house.'"*

Our gate hold time had nearly elapsed, so I started to go back to work on the radio. The funny thing about all these jokes was, that after each one, Lori and Diane would simultaneously recross their legs. They wouldn't say anything first, they would just do it. It was sort of like a drum roll at the end of each punch line.

Anyway, the girls recrossed their legs and Lori said, "Did you hear about the airline captain who won the $10 million lottery?"

We shook our heads, so Lori said, "He immediately called his wife and said, 'Pack your bags honey — I just won the lottery.'

"His wife said, 'Great! Should I pack warm clothes or cold weather things?'

"The captain said, 'Frankly darling, I don't give a damn — just so long as you're out of the house by the time I get home.'"

Well, I'll have to admit, they did make me laugh. Lori and Diane went back to the cabin to entertain the passengers with their simultaneous leg crossings while Abe and I prepared for the taxi sequence. I had to agree with Abe, when he said that if you had to be stuck on the gate at LaGuardia — that was the way to do it.

Fruits of the Nut Tree

Isn't it fun to run across old friends in unexpected places? That was what happened to me on my last trip. I was running up a jet way in San Francisco, when I bumped into Dan Phillopi (Dan and I used to fly C-141s together at Travis AFB).

The last time I saw Dan was about 8 years ago — he had to leave some course that he was attending at Altus AFB early, so he bequeathed his supply of BOQ-room food to me, (I still owe him a kitchen full of food).

Anyway, it had been so long since I had seen anyone from my old unit, that I asked him how some of the guys were doing. I was a little surprised at the answers, though I probably shouldn't be.

Dan used to own a Cessna 172 with two other guys in the squadron, Paul and Johnny Mac. Each one of them owned 1/3 of the airplane, and they ostensibly used it to fly to Lake Tahoe on the weekends to hunt and fish. They kept the airplane at the Nut Tree airport, which is just outside Vacaville, California.

Those three guys made for a pretty strange partnership. Before he got into that reserve unit at Travis, Johnny Mac used to fly H-46 helicopters in the Marine Corps. The reserve commanders at Travis didn't find out about his "early" discharge from the Marines until after he had gone through C-141 school, so they let him stay around to try to recoup some of their training investment. I'm sure there were times when they doubted the wisdom of that decision.

Johnny Mac got tanked up in Waikiki one night and told me the story about his discharge from the Marine Corps. The way he told it, his unit was bivouacked out in the desert somewhere near El Toro. A railroad track ran along the perimeter of their bivouac, and the train engineers were fond of blowing their whistles when they raced by at 2 in the morning.

The track ran straight and level for about 100 miles in that stretch of the desert, so the engineers would get their trains up to max speed by the time they sailed past the bivouac area. The Marine aircrews complained about the whistles, but no one seemed to be able to do anything about the situation.

About a week into the exercise, the opportunity to respond to the engineers presented itself while Johnny Mac was returning from a mission. Normally, he wouldn't have been flying into the bivouac area at that time of the night, but a mechanical problem earlier in the evening had delayed his return.

Johnny Mac made sure that since they were going to be late anyway, their arrival time would coincide with the nightly passage of the Southern Pacific. They loitered west of the field with their external lights off until they saw the single, warbling headlight of the train engine racing toward their bivouac area from the east.

Johnny timed their approach so that they would meet the train exactly abeam the Marines' bivouac area. When the time was right, he dove down until the H-46 was racing along about 10 feet over the twin steel rails at 90 knots. When they were about 10 miles from the train, Johnny Mac switched on the powerful search light mounted below the H-46, and began pivoting the beam around in a circle to emulate the headlight of train engine.

Of course the Southern Pacific engineer thought that he was racing toward another oncoming engine! The engineer laid down on the whistle, but it was obvious that their closing rate was too great for either engine to be able to stop. The engineer slammed on the brakes, and held down the whistle, and every Marine in the bivouac area awoke to a thundering, colossal shower of sparks sliding past their area at 70 miles-per-hour!

Johnny Mac kept up the ruse until the last possible second, when he pulled the helicopter's cyclic control stick back into his lap and zoomed over the whistling, sliding, sparking engine. When the engineer finally realized that the collision he was braced for had not occurred, he opened his eyes — and was astounded to see that the oncoming train had vanished!

Johnny's recollections of the rest of the story seemed to be a little distorted by the Mai Tais', but the best I could tell, there seemed to be some trouble between the Marine Corps and the Southern Pacific Railroad about some derailed rail cars, and Johnny wound up being asked to leave the Corps. It worked out best for everyone in the long run. Johnny fits in much better in the Reserves, and the Marine Corps still conducts exercises in that area to this day, with no problems from the Southern Pacific engineers.

Anyway, Johnny Mac joined the unit and convinced Paul to become a partner in the 172 with him. Paul was quite a piece of work in his own right.

Paul was one of those guys who always seemed to be going 100 mph in all directions at once — all airspeed and no heading. He was fun to be around though, because he *always* had something going on. It was tough to keep up with him — our commander always said that flying with Paul was like necking with a giraffe.

Paul's biggest frustration in life was the time he spent waiting for crew buses. Everytime I flew with him, we always called ahead and asked for a crew bus to meet our airplane, but inevitably we wound up having to wait half an hour for a bus to show up. He used to refer to that waiting time as "the period of maximum flustration."

Paul had a favorite joke that he liked to tell while we waited for the crew bus. It was the one about the Japanese car salesman who slowly started developing a terrible case of bad breath. No matter what he ate or how often he gargled and brushed his teeth, his breath still smelled awful. To make matters worse, he started experiencing sharp gas pains, which he could only relieve by passing startlingly-loud flatus.

As if that weren't enough, the flatus started making a very distinctive sound. Whenever he lifted his leg to relieve his pains, everyone in the room would swear that they heard someone grunting, "Hoonnddaaaaaa!"

It finally became too embarrassing for the salesman, so he went to a doctor to see if something could be done. It just so happened of course, that he went to a Japanese doctor, who asked him to demonstrate the phenomenon for him.

The salesman tightened his stomach muscles and raised his leg, and soon the doctor heard the unmistakable sound, "Hoonnddaaaaaa!"

The doctor asked the salesman to drop his pants, whereupon he examined his posterior. When he was finished, he stood in front of the salesman and asked him to breathe in his face. When he did, the doctor pronounced in his thick Japanese accent, "A ha! You have a zackery breath!"

The salesman said, "Zackery breath, what the heck is that?"

The doctor said, "Zackery breath mean — your breath smell zackery like your butt!"

The salesman said, "Can you cure it?"

The doc said, "Doctor can't cure zackery breath, you need a dentist."

So, the doctor recommended a good Japanese dentist friend of his, and soon the salesman was sitting in his examining chair. The dentist read through the doctor's report, then asked the salesman to demonstrate the strange flatus sound. Even the dental hygienist in the next room heard the loud, "Hoonnddaaaaaa!" that followed.

The dentist picked up his mirror and explorer, and began poking around inside the salesman's mouth. After about ten minutes, the dentist proclaimed, "Here it is — you have abscessed tooth!"

The salesman said, "An abscessed tooth is causing my bad breath?"

The dentist said, "Abscessed tooth causing both problems."

The salesman said, "What? How can that be true?"

The dentist said, "You never hear — *abscess makes the farts go Honda?*"

I admit — it helps to be stranded on a 110 degree ramp waiting for a crew bus to really appreciate that humor. But, that was Paul for you.

Paul was the guy who responded to the divert to Keflavik with a Bible quote. They were half way across the Atlantic when 21st Air Force called them on the HF radios and ordered them to divert into Iceland. Paul knew they were supposed to make the command post controllers authenticate whenever they received a divert order — but Paul's copilot had failed to pick up the "secrets" before they left Dover AFB.

So, Paul radioed back, "Authenticate Deuteronomy, Chapter 27, Verse 18."

It took them a few minutes to dig up a Bible, but the controllers were finally able to read the passage to him. Paul figured that not too many Russians would have a Bible handy while they were trying to trick him into diverting to Keflavick, so he accepted the order.

(The verse reads, "Cursed be he that maketh the blind to wander out of the way.")

Paul ran a little on the wild side, but not so much so that he would have partnered-up with Johnny Mac, if it hadn't been for Paul's girlfriend in Sacramento. Paul's first marriage was going through its final throes at that time, and he was secretly seeing a girl in Sacramento who later became his second wife.

His first wife was *extremely* jealous — *violently jealous.* So, Paul was always pretty nervous about the excuses he gave her for going to Sacramento. When Johnny approached him with the 172 partnership idea, Paul jumped at the chance to have a ready alibi for disappearing over long weekends.

Airplanes aren't cheap, so that's where Dan came in. Johnny Mac and Paul offered to let Dan in on the airplane, with the understanding that Johnny Mac and Dan would fly it to Tahoe on the weekends, and drop Paul off at Sacramento's Metro airport on the way.

Dan and Johnny would hunt and fish all weekend and then pick up Paul on their way home. They always split up their catch with Paul so he could take something home to his jealous wife to support his alibi, and everyone was happy.

Dan told me their arrangement finally ended one weekend a

couple of years ago because of a serious storm in the mountains. Johnny and Dan were supposed to leave Tahoe late Sunday afternoon and pickup Paul, but a storm at the lake kept them grounded. The snow was so bad that their 4-wheel drive jeep couldn't even make it out of the woods, much less to the airport.

Paul drove to Sac Metro at the appointed time and waited for the 172 to show up, but it never did. Dan and Johnny couldn't even get to a phone to call Paul and explain their tardiness.

Paul spent all night waiting for them at the airport. When Dan and Johnny finally showed up the next morning, a haggard Paul climbed into the back seat of the 172 and said, "Thank God you guys are alive — *I was scared to death you had crashed without me!*"

I asked Dan about Paul and Johnny Mac, and he said that both of them had left the Reserves. Apparently, they were both in the airplane that accidentally taxied into a crew bus in the Philippines a couple of years ago.

Paul knew that even though they were taxiing on the taxi line and following the marshallers' instructions, *they* would be hung for striking the unlighted crew bus on the dark ramp. So, when Paul wrote up the accident report, he and Johnny Mac gave the Air Force one last shot by writing, "We were taxiing into our parking spot, when we noticed that a crew bus was parked there, waiting for us. We were so surprised, that we ran over it."

Their resignations were included with the accident report.

But, all is well that ends well I suppose — Paul and Johnny Mac are happily employed by reputable airlines now, and Dan is no longer saddled with the expense of being one of the "Nut Tree Fruits."

It's fun to catch up on old friends, isn't it?

I Wish I'd Said That

I got to fly a trip today with Craig Hildebrant — it was fun catching up on all the things that had happened since the last time we had flown together.

The trip got off to a running start when an elderly lady passenger insisted on "seeing the captain" before she would sit down. Of course we couldn't push back from the gate until everyone was seated, so Craig told the "A" flight attendant, Becky, to bring the lady up front and he would talk to her.

When she entered the cockpit, the first thing she did was comment on Craig's youthful appearance. Craig did an excellent job of coming across as a sincere, concerned, professional; while he assured her that he held the highest possible pilot ratings, and had thousands of hours of flying experience.

Then, the lady said, "I haven't flown on an airplane in *fifty* years! But I do know something about airplane flying, because I flew on airplanes when very few people were willing to fly on them. You weren't even born when I flew on an airplane for the first time — did you know that?!"

Craig assured her that he believed everything she was saying, so she continued, "I remember very well, that the airplanes I flew on, had propellers on the front of the motors. Now I looked at the motors on this airplane, and I didn't see any propellers at all! Now what is going to make this airplane go — if it doesn't' have any propellers on the front of the motors?!"

Craig was still playing the professional airline captain very well when he answered, "Well mam, the engines on this airplane are *jet* engines, and they don't need propellers. They power the airplane with the thrust that they produce?"

The lady said, "The what?"

Craig said, "The thrust mam, the thrust."

It was readily apparent that the lady wasn't following his argument, so Craig tried to set her mind at ease with just enough of a semi-technical explanation, to make her feel like she could trust him.

Craig pointed to the start switches on the overhead console and said, "You see mam, when we push these buttons in, it makes those real sharp turbine blades that you can see in the front of the motors, spin around real fast."

Craig pointed to the start levers below the throttles and said, "Then, when I lift this start lever, it shoots fuel into the motor. That fuel is ignited, and that starts a fire inside the motor which is *real* hot. When the the air in between those sharp turbine blades, gets heated up by that fire — why it rushes out the back of the engine *real fast.*"

Craig paused to nod at the lady, to make sure she understood his explanation so far. Instead of nodding back, she looked him straight in the eye and said, "Why hell — so would anybody!"

I wish I had a picture of Craig's face when she said that. Fortunately, she was just as tired of listening to his explanations, as he was of giving them, so Becky was able to persuade her to take her seat. She insisted on sitting in the left window seat, in the last row. I assumed it was to check on Craig's story about thrusties rushing out the back of the motors.

The first leg of the trip took us to Philadelphia. We flew there at Flight Level 350 (35,000 feet), but shortly after we leveled off Craig told me not to be surprised if they asked us to climb to FL 370.

When I asked why, he told me, "Last week when I flew this trip, New York Center called us and said he needed us to climb to FL 370. We told him we were a little heavy to operate at that altitude, but he insisted that we climb immediately for 'Noise Abatement.'"

"I said, 'We're already at FL 330, what do you mean, noise abatement?'

"He said, 'I've got an opposite-direction Delta tri-star descending through your altitude at 12 o'clock — do you know how much racket that would make if you guys met nose to nose up there?'"

That got us started on the "quotable controller" stories, so I told him a couple of the stories that James F. MacNutt sent to me from Abbotsford, British Columbia.

Mr. MacNutt's 15-year scrapbook of controller stories included the tale of a young pilot initiating the following radio exchange:

32R: "Bellanca 32 Romeo — out of control."

Tower: "Frequency change approved."

As Mr. MacNutt put it, "The controller took quite a chance on this one; the pilot, with a poor choice of words, was simply stating that he was clear of the airport traffic area and signing off the frequency."

As an Oshkosh veteran, I also enjoyed his story about the poor soul trying to file a flight plan in that hectic environment, who finally resorted to calling Oshkosh tower and initiating the following exchange:

49L: "Hello Oshkosh tower, Bellanca 49L — I can't get Flight Service to answer me for a flight plan. Any ideas?"

Oshkosh tower (OSH): "He's probably out looking at clouds. Tell you what; call him again, and say 'FLIGHT-NO-SERVICE' see what happens."

49L: "Flight-no-watch already told me that — thanks anyway."

OSH: "Sure."

We could write an entire book on Oshkosh stories, but we can't mention one of them without telling the old OSH classic:

First time to OSH pilot: "Uh, Oshkosh tower, this is Goose 5558B, I'm over the gravel pit circling, and I got traffic behind me; what do I do?"

OSH: *"Well triple nickel eight-ball — if you can... keep him behind you!* If you look due east, you'll see a hundred and twenty-two airplanes on final — get behind the last one."

I enjoyed Mr. MacNutt's story about the first female first-officer's voice he heard on the radio while he was working tower frequency one morning. Instead of clearing her aircraft for a frequency change to departure control, he waited until he was fairly certain they had climbed above the overcast, then he pressed his mike button and said:

Tower: "Northeast 611, are you on top?"

The lady replied: "I'm always on top — I like it on top."

My favorite "MacNutt story" was his tale about the local wealthy businessman who wanted more than anything to solo an airplane, but he was scared to death of experiencing an engine failure in a single-engine airplane.

It didn't take his friends long to convince him that the light twins of the day were even more dangerous than the single-engine models. Most had just enough power with one engine operating to carry its unfortunate pilot to the scene of the crash, *if* he managed to avoid spinning to his death after decelerating below Vmca (minimum control airspeed).

The risks outweighed the gains in the businessman's mind, until Cessna introduced its push-me pull-me line of light twins which guaranteed sufficient center-line thrust to sustain flight on one engine. Finally, the businessman found what he had been waiting for, and he quickly coerced the owner of the first Cessna Skymaster in the area, into renting the aircraft to him long enough to solo in it.

Unfortunately, all the intricacies of airmanship can not be purchased quite as easily as tach time, and the businessman soon found that he either needed 8 more hands or 4 assistants in order to professionally pilot the Cessna about the traffic pattern with his present level of proficiency.

Mr. MacNutt, (manning the tower the day of the businessman's infamous solo flight) was somewhat bemused by the gentleman's habit of changing his call sign with each radio transmission. He understood that the amateur pilot was completely overwhelmed with the complexities of twin throttles, carb heats, prop controls, and fuel mixtures — so he assumed an understanding attitude when the businessman fouled-up his radio calls.

However, a couple of times the potential for disaster did evolve as a result of the businessman's changing call signs in the traffic pattern. At one such point, MacNutt attempted to clarify the situation with the following radio transmission:

Tower: *"Six-One-Delta,"* (MacNutt simply resorted to calling the businessman by the last call sign he had used) *"confirm that YOU'RE the Skymaster?"*

When the pilot of 61D was finally able to release the controls long enough to reply, he said: *"Uh, No sir—I'm only a student pilot."*

I had just finished telling Macnutt's stories when Becky opened the cockpit door and stepped inside with a pair of steaming coffees. After the cups were in their holders, Becky said, "You're not going to belive the message I have for you."

Craig said, "What's that?"

Becky said, "You remember the lady who wanted to know why there were no propellers on the engines?"

Craig said, "Yea?"

Becky said, "Well, she just told me to come up and tell you that you left your turn signal on."

Craig calmly told Becky to go back and reassure the lady that the flashing red light on the wing tip was supposed to be on, but I could tell he was starting to get a little upset. So, I tried to take his mind off of the lady by telling a story that Donald Aspinall sent to me.

Mr. Aspinall was a gunner in B-29s during WWII — he lives in Florida today. Mr. Aspinall wrote in his letter that they often told jokes over the intercom while they were flying bombing missions over Japan — it helped ease the tension a little bit while they waited for the Japanese Zero attacks.

Mr. Aspinall wrote that one of his favorites, was the story about the young aviation cadet flying a solo sortie one day at Graham AFB (since decommissioned).

The cadet was feeling particularly frisky that morning, so he began taunting the tower controllers with his radio calls, "Graham tower, this is Graham cracker — eat me."

He refused to identify himself when the tower demanded that he do so, and he continued the taunts intermittently throughout the morning (much to the delight of his class mates). Unfortunately, he played the joke out a little too long. He failed to keep track of how many aircraft were still in the pattern, and whether they were using calls signs that indicated they were dual or solo ships.

While flying downwind on his last pattern before making a full stop landing, the cadet decided to get in one more shot, so he trimmed-up his AT-6 and then transmitted, "Graham tower, this is Graham cracker — *EAT ME.*"

The tower controller calmly replied, "Graham cracker this is Graham tower, consider yourself eaten — you're the last solo ship in the air."

While we were on the subject of classic comebacks, Craig told me the one about the airline captain who objected to a 90 degree vector from approach control in order to get spacing on a light, private airplane.

The captain grabbed his mike and radioed, "Do you realize that it costs my company $300 every time I make a 90 degree turn with this 747?"

The controller answered, "Yes well, unfortunately while you were telling me that, you closed up on the Cessna ahead of you even more — make a $600 turn to the right now please."

My C-5 flying buddy in San Antonio, Hollywood Huggins, told

a similar version of that story that I liked. Hollywood's version had the captain answering the the controller's vector with the question, "Do you know how much it costs my company for me to do that?"

The controller answered, "No, I don't — but you could ask your first officer."

The key to winning these exchanges seems to be: "Whoever keeps their cool — wins."

Charlie Atwood told us about the irate female controller he heard on ground control in Dallas one morning, who provided an excellent example of this principle. Charlie said that this young lady started giving a Delta crew the full fury of her righteous scorn, after they asked her to repeat a radio transmission (her first transmission was "stepped-on" by another crew, calling for taxi clearance).

When she finally released her microphone button, a stunned silence hung over the airdrome at Dallas, as the pilots in dozens of cockpits marveled at the disdainful ferocity of her transmission.

After several seconds, the silence was finally broken by the drawling voice of the Delta flight's captain, asking, *"Excuse me honey... but have I ever been married to you?"*

As long as we're discussing ground control incidents, I might as well mention my old C-5 stick buddy, Ralph Lucas, and his story about the foggy morning he spent recently in Chicago. The O'Hare ground controller was attempting to manage the ramp traffic using model airplanes on his desk and scribbled notes on a legal pad, but it wasn't going well. He couldn't even see the airplanes that he was supposed to be controlling. Needless to say, he was soon swamped.

Finally, the situation snow-balled on him to the point that he needed to stop the entire operation, and regroup. So, with his frustration and anxiety readily evident in his cracking voice, the controller squeezed his mike button and said, "Break, break, break — everybody *stop* right where you are! Nobody move! Everybody stay off the radio! Don't move, and don't say anything — I'll call you as soon as I get this mess figured out!"

Ralph said that he waited patiently for several minutes in the cockpit of his American DC-10, and remarkably, everyone complied with the controller's wishes.

No one broke the ensuing silence for nearly 5 minutes, then Ralph heard a squeaky, nerdish-sounding voice on ground frequency saying, *"Eastern moved, Eastern moved."*

Of course sometimes actions speak louder than words, which was exactly the situation one day in Philadelphia when a Piedmont F-28 was told to taxi clear of the runway hold line to allow an airplane of "a competing carrier from the South" to go ahead of them.

The F-28 is equipped with a very effective speed brake in the tail of the plane. When the Fokker's speed brake is deployed by the pilot, it divides in half from its streamlined storage position, and the two halves extend horizontally into the slip stream to provide the desired drag.

On this particular occasion, the Piedmont captain improvised a new use for their high-drag device. As the Fokker's tail swung around toward the "competing carrier's" airplane, the captain opened the speed brake, and the first officer emitted a loud "raspberry" over the radio.

Craig had a couple of good stories about pilot come-backs that he had heard while flying into Philadelphia. One of them was the tale about the Eastern pilot who was instructed to hold 190 knots to the Whitman Bridge.

The Eastern pilot responded, "Say buddy, do you happen to know where Monkey World is — just north of Miami?"

The controller responded, "I live in Philadelphia — how would I know where Monkey World is in Miami?"

The pilot answered, "I live in Miami — how am *I* supposed to know where the Whitman Bridge is in Philadelphia?"

There was a long pause, then the controller said, "Ok, just hold 190 knots to the inner marker."

A different voice answered from the Eastern cockpit this time, "Okay... but do you want us to land or strafe?"

Along with replies that we wish we had been quick enough to think of, we occasionally say things in haste which we wish we hadn't. Such as the captain who looked over at his despondent copilot at approximately 100 knots during the take off roll, and tried to console him with, "Ah come on Bill — cheer up."

The copilot leaned forward and said, "Gear up" which was immediately followed by the captain's, "Wh*at the bleep*!?*"

I also enjoyed Linda Lebo's story about her first training flight as a flight attendant at Piedmont. Linda's classmate, Jane, was also training on the same flight. Linda said that the senior flight attendant on the flight was *very* senior, and she was particularly gruff with

Linda and Jane.

At one point in the trip, their itinerary included a flight between two cities which were very close to each other, so the senior flight attendant ordered Jane to make an announcement, telling the passengers that there would be no beverage service on that flight.

Jane was quite shy, and very afraid of ad libbing on the PA system. She did fine as long as she could just regurgitate their standard memorized spiels — but the thought of making up unrehearsed announcements was terrifying for her.

When Jane said that she couldn't make the announcement, the senior flight attendant threw a tantrum and said, "If you want to work for this airline you will learn how to ad lib on the public address system. We can't always tell you what to say. Sometimes you will have to think for yourself!

"Now get on that microphone, and tell those people that the next leg that we're scheduled to fly is too short for us to serve them!"

Jane hesitantly removed the microphone from its storage hook and turned away from the people, so they couldn't see the fear on her face as she spoke. She pressed down the mike button and said, "Ladies and gentlemen, we regret to inform you, that due to the short duration of this flight, we will be unable to serve you between our legs."

Of course, at other times, we can become so preoccupied with thinking of something cute to say, that we forget to take care of the business at hand. Such was the case in an incident that my friend John told me about, while he and his captain were flying their Air Cal (oops, I meant American) BAE-146 over the mountains of southern California.

John's captain's name was Jim Bob, and he was originally from Mississippi. In spite of living in San Diego for 19 years, Jim Bob still enjoyed affecting a deep southern drawl. He found that the California flight attendants were very fond of the accent.

One of the flight attendants on this trip was particularly beautiful, and Jim Bob made sure that he kept her in the cockpit as much as he could. He enjoyed making her laugh with his southern witticisms.

Jim Bob was busy inserting a last-minute change into his Jepessen charts while John flew. The gorgeous flight attendant sat behind their seats, giggling often at Jim Bob's flirtations.

They were experiencing a considerable amount of turbulence over the mountains, but Jim Bob was too preoccupied with their cockpit visitor to notice. John thought that it was a little too rough to be doing Jepessen changes, but he also assumed that Jim Bob might have an alternative reason for holding his approach chart book open in his lap. Jim Bob appeared to be *truly* enjoying the flight attendant's company.

Jim Bob finally got around to inviting the lady to his beach house in San Diego, and she replied something to the affect that a visit to his place would be nice, but what would they do there? The possible responses were truly arousing.

Had he been looking out the window instead of back at his date, Jim Bob would have realized that the lenticular cloud they were about to fly into would quite likely give them a significant jolt. But, Jim Bob was busy delivering his reply, "Honey, any time you feel like visiting my place — you can count on amusing yourself by dabbin your biscuits in the gravy of my heart."

The 146 was tossed up first, which immediately sent warning signals to Jim Bob, that all the pages in his open approach book were about to tossed around the cockpit. When the airplane stopped its sudden ascent and began sinking rapidly, Jim Bob lifted his knees and squeezed his legs together to try to keep his Jepessen charts from flying helter-skelter.

Unfortunately, the action of Jim Bob's legs resulted in the metal snap rings of his Jepessen binder closing on the portion of his anatomy least likely to enjoy the experience.

The shrill, painful cry the passengers heard coming from the cockpit momentarily drowned out the sound of all 4 engines. Jim Bob's romantic overtures were somewhat curtailed for the next few weeks.

That was one of the few times that I've heard a story about someone thinking up just the right witty comeback at precisely the right moment, and I did *not* think to myself, "I wish I'd said that."

Wee Willy and the Undertaker

An old Army buddy of mine breezed through San Antonio last week on his way to Corpus Christi, the infamous Willy Tubesing. Willy was ferrying a Cobra from Ft. Riley, Kansas to Corpus Christi, Texas to have the gun turret worked on.

It was sure great to see old Willy again. The last time I saw him was about 8 years ago in Germany. I awoke to find the rascal leaning over the other side of the bed, waking my wife up with a good-morning kiss! But that's another story.

I first met Willy at Ft. Ord, California in (circa) 1977. Willy was the new WO-2 in the unit who was fighting as hard as he could to keep from going to Cobra school. He succeeded for awhile.

Willy and I made a couple of memorable flights in OH-58s together before they finally carted him off to Ft. Rucker for Cobra school. As a matter of fact, Willy was the first guy I ever hit a tree with in a 58.

We were flying a simple little NOE (Nap Of the Earth) profile to sneak up on some simulated bad guys. Willy was flying from the left seat, while I navigated from the right seat. It was hot, so we had the forward doors removed.

Willy was easing the scout helicopter up the side of a ridge, toward a saddle where two huge pine trees resided. We certainly didn't want to hang around at the top of the ridge, so I told Willy, "Just slide through the saddle and turn right as you descend into the canyon on the other side."

Willy pressed the mike button on his cyclic control stick and answered, "Roger."

I suppose I expected Willy to slide the fuselage of the helicopter between the trees, with the rotor blades swinging over the tops of both of them. Whatever I expected, I was comfortable enough with it to bring my head back inside the cockpit, where I concentrated on reading the map and planning the rest of our route to the target.

Willy, on the other hand, decided that flying high enough for the rotor blades to pass over the trees would result in just a tad too much unhealthy exposure. So, he decided to fly the entire helicopter between the trees.

My first clue that something was amiss, was a bizarre, rapid, chopping sound. As a matter of fact, it sounded just like somebody had rolled up a newspaper, and was now busily trying to cram it through a large fan.

I looked up from the map, but we were already past the pine tree on Willy's side of the helicopter, which was the one we had taken a bite out of. I couldn't see anything amiss, but the air had taken on a distinct "fresh pine" aroma — as if an aerosol can of air freshener had suddenly *blown up* in the back of the 58.

Willy seemed highly amused at the sudden look of anxiety he saw on my face. He didn't help matters any by sniffing a couple of times, then saying, "Smells kinda, Christmasy — doesn't it?"

Unfortunately, I didn't have time to debate the seasonal affect with Willy, as a half dozen glints of sunlight on the opposing ridge informed us that we had been acquired by the bad guys. Willy immediately swung the 58 back toward the saddle, hoping to remask on the other side of the ridge before the bad guys solved their targeting problem.

I glanced back down at the map, quickly trying to come up with a game plan for Willy after we were through the saddle again. This time, the sound of the rolled up newspaper being crammed through the fan had a certain familiar ring to it. The noise was quickly followed by the now familiar scent of Pinesol, but this time there was a new twist.

The last time we went through the saddle, Willy had hit the tree on his side of the 58. The retreating blade on that side had thrown the severed branches back, behind our tail boom.

This time, Willy decided to give himself a little more room on his side, and he wound up hitting the same tree, which was now on *my* side of the helicopter, and exposed to the *advancing* rotor blade. Instead of throwing the branches behind us, the advancing blade started filling up the cockpit with with a green cloud of pine needles!

When we were clear of the saddle I stuck my head outside the cockpit and looked back at the pine tree. It looked like something out of cartoon — a huge slice was missing from its middle.

We thought we were going to get away with the incident without anyone finding out about it. But, when we tried to walk away from the helicopter later (back at the airfield) our crew chief yelled after us, "Hey sirs, did you guys hit anything out there?"

Willy shook his head and said, "Huh-uh, not that I remember."

The crew chief just pointed up to the rotor blade over his head. The outside dozen feet or so of the normally olive drab blade, looked like it had been repainted with a fresh coat of bright, pine-green paint!

Willy thought that incident might be enough to keep him out of Cobra school, but no real damage had been done (to the helicopter at least). So, a few months later, Willy found himself sitting in the back seat of a Cobra on a hot, Alabama afternoon.

The stories that made it back to us while Willy was away at Ft. Rucker, Alabama, always involved Willy trying some new scheme to try to get them to throw him out of the school — but not ruin his career. Among other stories, we heard that he faked a sports injury that put him so far behind his class that he hoped they would send him home (at that time, if you didn't finish a course by the end of the fiscal year in which its funds had been appropriated, it presented special budgeting problems for the home unit).

Instead of shipping him home though, those wily Ft. Rucker IPs (Instructor Pilots) worked out a special syllabus whereby Willy could catch up with his class. Their accelerated syllabus required Willy to fly *four* sorties each day during the gunnery/tactics phase of the course, instead of one.

Willy's IP (Jack Berry) wasn't too happy about the accelerated program either. So, by the end of the syllabus, he was also looking for creative ways to abbreviate the course. Which, explains why he said what he did, as Willy hovered their Cobra along the NOE route which lead from the FARRP (Forward Area Rearm & Refuel Point) to the gunnery range.

The standard syllabus involved a long, drawn-out NOE attack profile, which began with the Cobra student hovering along an abandoned log road (which served as their NOE route) leading from the FARRP to the range. The combat engineers had positioned an APC (Armored Personnel Carrier) at the end of the log road, which the student was expected to use for "initial cover" when he approached the range.

After hiding behind the APC for a few moments, the student would "unmask" to one side of the APC, in order to select a target downrange. After selecting his potential target, the student would remask behind the APC, while he selected the target's most efficient method of destruction.

The Cobra students' choices normally ranged between a wide assortment of mini-gun, cannon, and rocket armament. This particular phase of the training syllabus, however, placed exclusive emphasis on 2.75-inch, folding-fin rocket attack.

To meet this training objective, Willy's Cobra had been loaded exclusively with 2.75 inch rockets. There were two, 18-shot rocket pods under each wing, for a total of 72 rockets!

Berry had already watched Willy perform the attack ritual 3 times that day. Willy had selected one pair of marking rockets, unmasked again on the opposite side of the APC, and fired on his target. After making whatever sighting corrections were necessary after the impact of the marking rockets, Willy selected an appropriate number of rockets for the target, (half-tracks require a few more than motorcycles) and proceeded to blow it away.

The program would normally continue with a dash to a new cover area, selection of a new target, and it's stealthy destruction, until all 72 of the high-explosive rockets were expended.

Since this was their fourth sortie that day, Berry was less-than-enthusiastic about sweating off any more pounds that afternoon, just to observe Willy's obvious prowess in "rocket-slingin".

Anyone who has ever spent any time in the green house that they call a cockpit on a Cobra, can readily understand why Berry pressed his floor mike button as Willy approached the end of the log road and asked, "Say Willy, have you salvoed a complete load of rockets yet?"

When Willy wants to let you know that he understands what you're trying to write for him between the lines, he can turn a "No" answer into a three syllable reply.

When Berry heard Willy's response, he smiled to himself, then pressed his mike button again and said, "Well, it's an important aspect of rocketry which you really should experience. You can certainly unload a lot of weight in a hurry that way if you need to for some performance reason (such as an engine failure) and it's important for you to understand the dispersion pattern that you're going to get if you fire all of the rockets at once."

Willy saw the opportunity Berry was offering, so he immediately said, "Sounds good to me — can we try it on this ride?"

They were rapidly approaching the end of the log road. The "initial cover" APC was already in sight, a scant 50 yards ahead.

Berry knew they were running out of time, so he said, "Sure, just set your fire selector switch to the salvo position, and fire at the APC."

Now, the effective shrapnel radius of a 2.75 inch rocket is well over 50 yards. So, what Berry actually *meant* to say was, *When we get to the APC...* unmask, and fire all of the rockets."

Willy, on the other hand, had already surmised that the secret to success in the Cobra transition course, was to do *exactly* what the IP said. It looked a bit close to Willy, but, he twisted the fire selector knob to the "salvo" detent, bit his bottom lip, and pointed the Cobra's nose directly at the APC.

Berry's first clue that something was wrong, was the rapid-fire, "Whoosh, whoosh, whoosh, whoosh" on both sides of the aircraft as all 72 of the high-velocity rockets ignited!

The first pair of rockets had scarcely slammed into the thin armor of the APC before Berry started scrunching down in his seat — trying to make himself as small as possible behind the Cobra's ridiculously narrow, non-armored nose.

The sudden appearance of numerous holes in the plexiglass canopy and several red lights on the aircraft-systems' warning panel, convinced Willy that it was time to follow his IP's lead.

Nobody really flew the gunship for the next minute or so, it just sort of settled to the ground all by itself, amidst a hail of smoke, shrapnel, and APC components. When the crap finally (literally) stopped coming through the fan — Berry provided Army aviation with one of those memorable quotes they're so fond of.

He crawled up out of his tiny fetal position, looked out at the smoking pile of debris that used to be an APC, then twisted around so he could look at Willy and said... "I think you got him Willy."

Needless to say, we greatly enjoyed the astonished looks that appeared on the face of Willy's copilot (a brand new WO-1 named Mike) as we relived those old stories. After all, for the entire time that Mike had known Willy — Willy had been WO-4 "Dr. Death" Tubesing.

We probably would have stayed up all night providing Mike with black-mail material for when they got back to Ft. Riley — but sometime around midnight, my 14-year-old blender gave up the ghost. After a few moments of silence (in respect for the blender's smoke-and-spark filled demise) we packed it in for the night.

The next morning, Brenda treated the crew to a hearty San Antonio breakfast of home-made chorizo & egg breakfast tacos, fried potatoes, and coffee — then I drove Willy and Mike back to Kelly AFB to retrieve their Cobra. There was some trouble over their fuel credit card, but Willy resolved the problem while Mike preflighted their bird, and they were finally ready to continue their sojourn south.

I was just getting ready to say my good-byes, when Willy asked, "How long has it been since you've flown a Cobra?"

"About ten years," I answered.

"Think you still remember how?" he challenged.

Mike was observing this entire exchange, so I felt compelled to put up a good show of bravado. I put my hands on my hips and said, "I'm pretty rusty — I probably couldn't do any better than you right now."

This behavior is typically described as, "Writing checks with your mouth that your butt can't cash," since the truth is that I never could outfly Tubesing, even when I was current in helicopters.

Willy smiled like a cat looking at a clipped parrot, then he waved his arm at Mike and said, "Why don't you let Sherm borrow your survival vest for a minute — we'll be right back."

Well, I happened to be wearing my multi-zippered frog suit anyway (since I was planning to fly a C-5 local after I saw Willy and Mike off) so I readily welcomed the chance to fly a Cobra around the pattern again. I strapped myself into the front seat and Willy cranked up the helicopter and hovered us out to the runway.

Willy gave me the controls and obtained take off clearance from the tower, and seconds later I was reliving the thrill of *lowering* the nose and accelerating into the sky. I'll be honest with you — just flying that ship around the pattern and down the runway in a high-speed pass, was the biggest rush I've felt since my first T-38 ride.

The feel of those side-arm controls, the fantastic visibility from that forward cockpit, the powerful chop of the blades — it opened up a dozen adrenal glands that had been in remission for years. I could feel the spurs growing out of the heels of my flight boots.

The tower cleared us for a second closed pattern, and as I pulled the gunship up into a climbing left turn, I remembered a question that I had intended to ask Willy the previous evening (before the blender tragedy).

When we were stabilized on what tower told us would be an extended downwind leg, I pressed the intercom button on the cyclic and said, "Say Willy, do you have any idea about what happened to old Don Collins from Ft. Ord?"

Even without his mike button depressed, I could hear Willy laughing in the back seat. When he finally composed himself enough to speak, he said, "Yea, Don's at Ft. Riley with me! Did you hear about his incident at Ft. Carson?"

I answered, "No, I haven't heard anything at all about him since he left Ft. Ord back in 1979."

Willy said, "Well, Don married a young lady who is quite an artist. She makes beautiful Christmas ornaments every year, and last year she got an idea for some ornaments made out of pine cones.

"The problem is, we don't have too many pine cones around Ft. Riley, Kansas. So, last November, when she learned that we were being sent on an exercise to Ft. Carson, Colorado — she was ecstatic!

"She told Don to keep his eyes open for pine cones, and bring home as many as he could cram into his Cobra — the bigger, the better!

"By the last day of the exercise, Don had collected a dozen bags filled with pine cones, but he didn't have any really big ones. He and a guy named Perigo were flying gun cover for a Huey (that was supposed to pick up a radio team from the top of a mountain) when Don glanced down and saw the biggest pine cone he had ever seen in his life.

"Don was flying in the front seat of his Cobra, so he immediately called the Huey and said, 'Hey guys, wait a minute — I need to circle back and grab that monster pine cone we just flew over.'

"The Huey drivers were buddies of his who knew what he was up to, so they circled back and watched while Don brought the Cobra to a hover beside this pine tree. The pine cone Don was after was hanging from a limb right at the top of the 70-foot tree. There was no place to set down, so Don's plan was for Perigo to hover the Cobra next to the tree, while he opened his canopy and snatched the cone off the limb.

"Don still had his intercom selector set to the FM radio position, so the Huey drivers heard him transfer the controls to Perigo so he could open his canopy.

"After he locked the canopy up, the Huey pilots heard Don using his floor mike button to vector Perigo in close enough to the tree so he could grab the cone. The Cobra hovered closer and closer to the trunk of the tree with its rotor blades swinging over its top branches, until Don was finally close enough to unfasten his shoulder harness and lean outside.

"Don had just placed his hands on either side of the cone, when the Huey crew heard his voice over the radio again. His single-word transmission summed up their tactical situation perfectly — he screamed, *'Bees!'*

"It's too bad the Huey drivers didn't catch the flight maneuvers that followed on tape, it would have provided an excellent example of evasive maneuvering. No gunner in the world would have been able to hit that gyrating Cobra as Don and Perigo alternated between swiping at the swarm of bees they had invited into their cockpit, and intermittently regaining control of the helicopter long enough to point it at a different impact site."

It would have been difficult enough for me to bring the Cobra to a hover without anyone talking — it didn't help matters any that Willy told the punch line while I was doing it. But, we survived, and I found myself handing Mike's survival vest back to him while Willy guarded the controls from the back seat.

I climbed up and shook hands with Willy while Mike strapped himself into the front seat. I couldn't see his eyes behind his sun visor, but I could read his smile. A few minutes later, I watched them disappear to the south.

My flight suit was soaked with sweat by the time I finished walking to my van for the drive to the other side of the airfield, and I knew I had to hang around for 3 hours before brief time for my C-5 local. But, if lightning had struck me as I climbed into my van — it would have taken the undertaker 3 days to wipe the smile off my face.

Retention Test...

Can you place the stories?

Mabel

Young Mabel from far-off Mt. Shasta,
Was marking her chart in Nebraska.
Her route was to Wooster,
But somebody goosed her,
And Mabel wound up in Alaska.

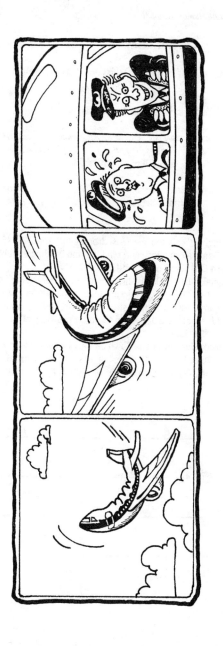

Oh no... Say it isn't so!

Tell me that you didn't really miss the book that started all of this...
The Aviation Humor of 1987.

Listen to what these readers had to say...

"By far the funniest stories I've ever heard. Once I opened it, I couldn't put it down. Thanks for making me laugh so much!"
Jane White—Danville, Il

"I loved it—my wife threw me out of bed I was laughing so hard!"
Robert Sadler—Bedford, Oh

Fortunately, it's not too late. Just drop a check for $7.45 ($5.95 + $1.50 P/H) into an envelope and send it to the Pendragon Publishing Co., 1484 Old Tara Ln., Ft. Mill, SC 29715

Please make the check payable to Pendragon Publishing Co.

There are three ways of ordering these books. You can write down your name, address, and desired book title, and slip it into the envelope with your check, or you can tear these pages out of this book to use as an order form.

Or, you could lay this book down on top of a copy machine and copy pages 126 & 127... and use the copy as your order form!

Incidentally, *The Aviation Humor of 1987* is NOT a children's book.

Your Name: _____

Street Address: _____

City & State: _____

Zip Code: _____

Satisfaction Guaranteed

The Little Apple Orchard

Listen to what these professional people have to say about this
high-quality children's book:

*My favorite book to read out loud to the class. They learn so much
about human nature from the exciting story line, and they love all
14 full-page illustrations.*
> Mary Van Nest—**Teacher**—San Antonio, Tx

*The kids always act more mature—more street smart, after they
read this book. They always read it more than once.*
> Kathy Gorena—**Librarian/Teacher**—San Antonio, Tx

*Very educational. My kids' favorite book to read together at
bedtime.*
> Pamela Williams—**Mother/Sunday School Teacher**—Hot
> Springs, Ar

*I liked it as much as my sons did. Great story, and outstanding art
work.*
> Les Harris—**Airline Pilot**—Waco, Tx

Make your check or money order for $7.00 ($4.95 + $2.05
postage & handling) payable to: Pendragon Publishing Co.
Address: 1484 Old Tara Ln., Ft. Mill, SC 29715

Your Name: _____

Street Address: _____

City & State: _____

Zip Code:_____

Satisfaction Guaranteed

ABOUT THE AUTHOR

Sherman Morgan began his aviation career as an Army helicopter pilot. He graduated from Army flight school at Ft. Rucker, Alabama in July, 1976. He was a Warrant Officer. He was stationed at Ft. Ord, California until July, 1979.

After completing his Army tour, Sherman joined the Air Force Reserve at Travis AFB, California, where he flew C-141 Starlifters. Later, he transitioned to the C-5 Galaxy. He flew C-5s at Travis AFB, California, Dover AFB, Delaware, and Kelly AFB, Texas. He has recently joined the C-130 Air National Guard unit at Charlotte, N.C.

Sherman currently resides close to Lake Wylie, South Carolina, with his wife of 17 years, and their 10 year old daughter.

Sherman flies for US Air from their Charlotte, North Carolina hub.

When he isn't flying, Sherman enjoys collecting stories for his humor books. He is currently working on *Classic Aviation Humor—Book III*. If you have a humorous flying story, write it down and mail it to the publisher. You will be given credit for the story if used in the next book.

ISBN 0-944792-01-4

50595

9 780944 792018